# Superstitions and Hekate

*Unlocking the Mysterious Realm of Supernatural Beliefs, Symbols, and Ancient Greek Magic*

# Your Free Gift
# (only available for a limited time)

Thanks for getting this book! If you want to learn more about various spirituality topics, then join Mari Silva's community and get a free guided meditation MP3 for awakening your third eye. This guided meditation mp3 is designed to open and strengthen ones third eye so you can experience a higher state of consciousness. Simply visit the link below the image to get started.

https://spiritualityspot.com/meditation

Or, Scan the QR code!

# Table of Contents

# Part 1: Superstition

*The Ultimate Guide to Superstitions, Signs, Omens, Symbols, Fortune Telling, Myths, Folklore, and History*

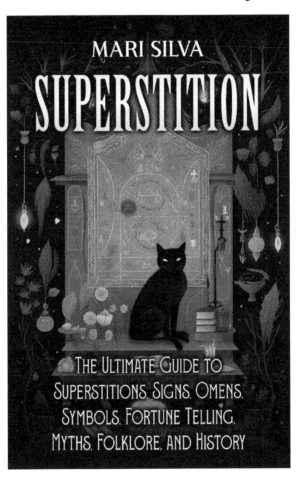

# Introduction

This book will take you on a journey through the fascinating world of superstitions, myths, and omens. For as long as humans have existed, we've looked for meaning in the world around us, and this has led to the creation of a rich and varied tapestry of beliefs and practices. Throughout the ages, we've looked to the sky, the earth, and the animals and plants around us, seeking signs and symbols that might help us make sense of the world. We've turned to fortune-tellers and diviners to try and see into the future, and we've used objects, food, and even numbers to bring luck and ward off misfortune. From the ancient belief in omens to the modern-day practice of Feng Shui, we've turned to these beliefs to help us navigate the ups and downs of life.

But why do we believe in these things? What about the human psyche makes us so susceptible to superstition? This book will answer this question by exploring the psychological and cultural factors that contribute to our belief in superstitions and examining the role fear, uncertainty, and the need for control have shaped our beliefs. You'll understand how people's upbringing, environment, and life experiences shape their beliefs and practices.

You will also get to take a closer look at the role of nature and the environment in our superstitions. The shapes of clouds, the patterns of bird flights, and the colors of the sky all hold meaning and significance in cultures around the world. Similarly, the behavior of animals and the properties of plants have been used to predict the future, offer protection, and even help with healing. You can also study the many different ways that superstitions have been used throughout history, from the ancient civilizations of Egypt and Greece to the modern-day world of horoscopes and lucky charms. Keep reading to explore the fascinating symbolism of colors, animals, and numbers, and delve into the many different superstitions around objects, food, and even birth and death.

Overall, this book offers a comprehensive look at the world of superstitions, myths, and omens; by its end, you'll have a deeper understanding of this rich and complex world. Whether you're a skeptic or a true believer, you will find something intriguing and thought-provoking in these pages. So, if you're ready to explore this mystical world and unlock the secrets of our collective beliefs, this book is the perfect place to start.

# Chapter 1: Why Do We Believe in Superstitions?

With the technological advancements and scientific discoveries of today's day and age, it is hard to believe that many people still strongly believe in seemingly irrational superstitions. However, you might be surprised to learn about the self-fulfilling nature of these beliefs and the psychology behind them. Nearly all superstitions practiced in different parts of the world today stem from interesting pieces of lore, stories, and myths. Some of them even seemed perfectly rational and useful at the time of their creation.

This chapter will set out to demystify what superstitions are and that they are *not just* sayings that your granny dropped into any conversation as a cautionary tale. We'll delve deep into why many superstitions appear true – even though they aren't backed by scientific evidence. You'll understand why many people believe in them and how individuals who don't believe in omens and good luck charms can become superstitious too!

This chapter also explores some of the most internationally widespread superstitions, explains where and how they originated, and highlights the differences and similarities of superstitions across cultures. You will learn how anthropologists define superstitions, why they study them, and how they classify them. Finally, you'll understand the interconnected nature of superstitions, myths, and folklore and how they can give us insight into how people used to think, act, and interact with the world around them.

# What Are Superstitions?

Have you ever walked into an elevator and found that the building has a 12B, 14A, or M floor rather than a 13th? Was the last plane you took missing a 13th or 17th row?

Were you ever told that you shouldn't have an early birthday celebration? How would people react if you opened an umbrella indoors? Do you hear the words "break your mother's back" ringing in your ears every time you accidentally step on a crack?

The number 13 is considered unlucky in most parts of the world, while the number 17 carries the title of "bad luck" in Brazil, Italy, and a few other countries. It is also generally believed that early birthday wishes and celebrations and the act of opening an umbrella indoors will attract bad luck.

These are all superstitions you've heard all your life, regardless of how superstitious you or your family are. They are commonly held beliefs that everyone follows despite not knowing the real reason behind them.

There isn't a single definition that can be attributed to the word superstition. It is a way of thinking and refers to how people perceive certain events and happenings. Superstitious people generally believe in fate, luck, and other supernatural forces and associate them with particular symbols or happenings. Superstitious individuals generally feel the need to reduce feelings of uncertainty by finding ways to predict the unknown. This means that an individual's personal beliefs and experiences shape their superstitions, which they would then accidentally or intentionally pass on to their children.

For instance, if you notice that you seem to have the best day at work whenever you see a butterfly on your way there, your brain's reward system will get activated each time you come across a butterfly. You'll automatically expect your day to go smoothly, and so will subconsciously do everything in your power to make it happen.

On the other hand, if you believe in the black cat superstition and come across one in the morning, you'll automatically assume that your day is ruined. Even if you don't necessarily self-sabotage, you won't do anything to give yourself a good day, either. If you run into problems or conflicts -expected in any work environment - you won't do anything to fix them because "it would be of no use." If you face problems when you're expecting things to work out for the best, this will encourage you to take positive remedial actions. Superstitions are self-fulfilling because people's beliefs influence their attitudes and behaviors, which shape their actions.

You might also start believing in a superstition just because someone pointed it out. Say you're heading out to work, and your neighbor warns you about the crow sitting at your windowsill all morning. He claims that crows are bad luck and that you must watch out. You brush it off, but it still lingers in your mind. There's traffic on your way to work, and you arrive late to an important meeting. You tell yourself this can happen to anyone and put it behind you. Then, you get into an argument with your co-worker, and to top it all off, you take the wrong exit on your way home – and now you have to spend an extra 30 minutes on the road! Normally, you'd tell yourself that everyone has bad days. However, now that you know that the crow you saw in the morning attracts bad luck, you might start to believe that the superstition is true.

## Why Do People Believe in Superstitions?

Each culture, or even family, has its own superstitions ingrained into the minds, behaviors, and daily interactions of its people. Some superstitions are even popular on a global level. If there is no scientific backing to these beliefs and associations, why do so many people believe in them?

Superstitious beliefs and behaviors can generally imbue a sense of direction and control in those who engage in them. The thought that the future, whether long- or short-term, is highly unpredictable makes many people feel anxious. To them, using external factors and occurrences to gain insight into the future or influence certain results helps them feel at ease. This explains why most superstitions originated during periods of wars, calamities, and economic crises, which cause feelings of uncertainty to arise among people.

According to The Conversation academic article, superstitious individuals are more likely to develop positive mental attitudes. They're also prone to making irrational decisions led by notions like fate and good or bad luck.

Superstitious people don't only look for signs in the outside world, but they also believe that they can do certain things to attract good fortune. For instance, they might carry charms, wear certain jewelry or clothes, or prefer specific numbers or colors on important days or when making significant decisions. They might also avoid doing specific things or wearing certain items altogether because they associate them with bad luck.

# Superstitions in the World of Sports

Superstitions are very popular in sports, especially when things get competitive. You might be surprised that around 80% of athletes follow superstitious regimens before competing. Most athletes find that these behaviors help reduce their anxiety and stress and give them a better sense of control over the outcome and factors beyond their control.

Even though each player and game has their own particular superstitions, there are commonalities. For instance, equestrians and gymnasts think they'll feel and appear more prepared when they look well-dressed and put together. Footballers and other athletes might pray for good outcomes. Many athletes also engage in personal superstitions, such as wearing lucky clothes or carrying charms around. Some players also dedicate certain sporting gear to competitions.

If you're into basketball, you might already be aware of Michael Jordan's superstitious behaviors. He wears lucky shorts under his team's kit. Björn Borg, the world-renowned tennis player, was known to wear the same branded shirts. Rafael Nadal also follows a pre-game ritual that helps boost his performance.

While these rituals won't directly steer the outcomes in the athletes' favor, they can actually help them perform better. Since said rituals and practices can help ease anxiety and make athletes feel more empowered, they'd be able to focus better on their performance than their thoughts and feelings. Stress and anxiety are known to hinder people's performance. If an athlete fails to engage in their superstitious behaviors before they perform, they'll feel anxious and worried, which then becomes evident on the scoreboard.

# Internationally Widespread Superstitions

Even though the general idea and structure of certain superstitions are shared by many countries worldwide, the meaning behind them and the consequences that follow if engaged with them might vary.

The following are some internationally widespread superstitions, their origins, and their similarities and differences across cultures:

## Touch/Knock on Wood

In many cultures worldwide, people believe that touching or knocking on a piece of wood can help free them of bad luck or attract good fortune. The phrase touch or knock on wood originated in 19th-century Britain, with little information on the story behind it. However, most explanations point back to the Celts, who thought trees served as homes for deities and other celestial creatures. The Celts thought that knocking on trees was a way to show gratitude to the spirits in exchange for abundance or to call on them for guidance and protection. Some people believe this practice also helped them get rid of bad luck and keep evil spirits from finding out about people's abundance so they wouldn't reverse their good fortune. The act of touching or knocking on wood can also be traced back to Christianity, as many historians suggest that wood is associated with the cross of Christ's crucifixion.

Many others suggest this superstition doesn't go that far back in history. According to Steve Roud, a British folklorist, the act of touching wood came from a 19th-century game of tag. In Tiggy Touchwood, children who touched any piece of wood during the game couldn't be caught by the other players. With the growing popularity of the game among both children and adults, wood became known as a source of protection, and therefore, the phrase "touch wood" was incorporated into the British vernacular.

While no one knows where the superstition came from, it is still among the most popular shared beliefs worldwide. Many cultures even have their own spin on the practice. For instance, in addition to knocking on wood twice, Turkish people tug at their ears to fight off jinxes, and in Italy, people say "touch iron" rather than wood when they're tempted to partake in risky behaviors.

## Toasting with Water

According to the Mess Night Manual of naval history, people who toast using a glass of water will die by drowning. Along with water, soft drinks and liqueurs can bring bad luck. This superstition can also be traced back to Greek mythology, as ancient Greeks avoided toasting with water out of respect to the River Lethe. Legend says that those who die sail to the Underworld via this river, so toasting with water would imply that you wish death by drowning on yourself or those you are toasting. Ancient Greeks also thought that using a glass vessel of water while toasting was an invitation to the deities to cast a series of bad luck upon you. The act of clicking a glass of water is practiced by many cultures to this day.

## Black Cats and Birds

Black cat.

Unfortunately, many widespread superstitions impact the lives of other innocent creatures. Black cats, for instance, were found to have lower adoption rates than cats of other colors. They're also often treated differently, discriminated against, overlooked, and even abused due to superstitions that they are carriers of bad luck. These beliefs are most pronounced around Halloween, as the poor furry animals are associated with witches. Many people around the world believe that their day will take a turn for the worse if they come across a black cat.

Black cats, however, are not the only creatures linked to bad omens. For example, South Koreans strongly believe that spotting a black crow would immediately result in bad fortune, and they also think they're messengers of death. In the UK, ravens are believed to predict impending doom. There's another superstition that the British monarchy will fall if the number of ravens spotted on the Tower of London, at any given moment, is less than 6. Scottish and Irish people think that ill fortune will come their way if they see a single magpie; however, they believe they're good to go if they come across two or more of this type of bird.

# How Anthropologists Classify Superstitions

Anthropologists study superstitions and the history behind them to gain insight into the differences between cultures, understand how people think, and learn more about the different ways individuals try to make sense of the world around them. Anthropologists are interested in discovering how and why these beliefs and perceptions are passed down from one generation to another.

They define superstitions as beliefs and practices not supported by logical or rational reasoning or scientific evidence and are purely shaped by group or individualistic beliefs, experiences, or traditions. They also generally classify superstitions into three categories: interpreting signs, magic superstitions, and conversion superstitions. How superstitions are classified depends on the relevant practices, behaviors, beliefs, and eminence in a cultural context. In most cases, superstitions are classified as aspects of larger spiritual or religious systems. However, some people think they aren't elements of organized belief systems.

Interpreting signs and superstitions refer to superstitious beliefs and practices that are content-based. These superstitions require interpreting and analyzing events, occurrences, symbols, or signs as omens of bad or good fortune. An example of this type of superstition would be carrying a horseshoe around to attract good fortune.

Magic superstitions are associated with practices and rituals used to attract good fortune and steer bad luck away. An example of this type of superstition would be carrying a charm to protect yourself from evil forces and harm or performing a certain ritual before tests or competitions to steer the results in your favor.

Conversion superstitions refer to the idea that a certain happening or practice can undo bad luck or convert it into good fortune. For instance, a superstitious person who steps on a crack in the sidewalk would take it as a sign of imminent bad luck. However, they might throw salt over their shoulder to attract good luck and cancel out the previous omen.

Anthropologists are careful to account for the social and cultural contexts in which the superstitions occur because even if the practices are the same across different cultures, their meanings may differ. They also observe the roles they play in the lives of people and the amount of influence that these superstitions have over their actions.

# How Superstitions, Myths, and Folklore Are Interconnected

The terms superstitions, myths, and folklore are often used interchangeably, which is why many think they all refer to old, whimsical tales. These terms indeed feature imaginative characters and storylines; however, they all aim to fulfill a significant purpose: to explain the world and answer the fundamental questions of life.

Back then, people didn't have the knowledge and technology to make sense of the world around them. They didn't understand why basic phenomena occurred, so they had to find other ways to explain them. They didn't realize that droughts were caused by environmental changes, for instance, and therefore assumed that they'd upset the god of rainfall. They didn't know the reasons behind their ailments, so blaming it on the black crow they'd seen earlier seemed reasonable at the time.

Each of these terms has unique characteristics; however, they're all similar in how their significance hasn't withered with time. They're also connected in how they transmit cultural traditions, values, ideologies, practices, and beliefs across generations. They each preserve cultural elements differently, giving insight into how people used to think and act and reflecting how individuals used to approach and interact with the world around them. You can tell a lot about a culture by reading into its myths and folklore and exploring its superstitions.

## How Are They Different?

Myths are traditional tales that provide answers to basic questions that people have about life, creation, and the world. They were commonly shared orally in efforts to explain supernatural happenings, certain phenomena, and mysteries. They were also used to back up cultural traditions and reinforce norms and values among people. Myths that revolved around deities and other spiritual creatures were sacred and still influence several aspects of many cultures to this day. They often explained certain events in light of spiritual beliefs, such as the occurrence of misfortunes due to upset gods or conflicts between them.

Myths and the personages featured in the myth influence many superstitions, such as toasting with water. Superstitions are merely elements of myths and are influenced by them – the terms are not interchangeable. While the former are traditional stories that comprise characters and events, superstitions are beliefs that *might or might not* have been featured in myths.

While myths often revolved around deities and explained how cultures and peoples originated, folklore revolved around people and other living creatures. Mythologies explored life through a spiritual lens, and folktales captured the essence and commonalities of daily life. Folklore gives us information about how people used to live. These tales explore common challenges and conflicts that people faced at the time and what they did to cope. Superstitions are popular elements in cultural stories and folktales.

Now that you have read this chapter, you understand why many people, regardless of how well-educated and intelligent they are, still believe in superstitions and allow them to influence various aspects of their lives. Superstitious practices give people a greater sense of control over their lives and help alleviate their anxiety toward unpredictable situations. Superstitions generally offer a sense of comfort and security. Many cultures also use these beliefs as ways to introduce and develop cultural values and norms. Superstitions are double-edged swords. They are mind tricks that can either encourage us to work hard or succumb to the status quo. Hard work brings good fortune, so don't fret the next time you are seated in the 13th row or step on a crack in the sidewalk.

# Chapter 2: Superstition and Fortune-Telling

Fortune telling refers to the craft used to interpret the future or identify the influences of past and present actions. It's also part of a larger group of practices called divination. The latter is used to unveil hidden knowledge through magic and intuitive awareness. While the concepts of divination and fortune-telling are often used interchangeably, divination often reveals information on a much larger scale. Nevertheless, both fortune-telling and divination are often linked to superstition. This chapter explores the connection between divination and superstition. It also provides popular and simple divination methods suggested for beginners, including tea-leaf reading, scrying, tarot reading, and automatic writing.

## The Connection between Superstition and Fortune Telling

Fortune-telling involves looking for meaning in patterns and symbols. Many of these patterns came from observing nature and the causes of the events in nature. Even in ancient times, people were closely affiliated with nature and what it was doing and trying to make sense of it. While (to the untrained eye) it might seem impossible to make sense of random patterns, the unconscious mind is very good at finding meaning even when there seemingly isn't any. A great example is people's ability to see faces and other images in living beings and non-living objects around them. This phenomenon is responsible for the birth of many superstitions too. When seeing something they couldn't interpret, people found alternate interpretations for shapes and symbols and linked them to known objects with similar characteristics. Throughout history, the working and lower classes often could not conceive the reasoning behind misfortunes and other sudden events. Since these seemingly inexplicable events made them feel that they don't have control over their lives, they simply found a different explanation for them, thereby taking back the desired control. Whatever signs or symbols they noticed just before the events were linked to the newfound explanations. If their subconscious associates an object or animal with a particular event, they interpret seeing the latter as a sign of that event, which is also just how fortune telling or divination in general works.

## Symbols and Fortune Telling

Whichever divination method you use, being a fortune teller enables you to become a medium through which you gather information. You can garner knowledge about yourself or someone else seeking information about their future, present or past. For beginners, start practicing by divining for yourself first before you undertake to guide others. This will give you the experience of building a connection between your tools, that is, the method of choice and your intuition. Whether seeking information about love, finances, or spirituality, you'll need to learn how to fine-tune your readings.

In this chapter, you'll be given several techniques, each requiring you to decipher messages by looking for shapes and symbols. Whatever you see will create a symbolism in your mind, which will help form a connection between the explanation in your unconscious mind and the image in your conscious mind. This connection is the key to deciphering divinatory messages. In the subsequent chapter, you'll read about the symbolism of different superstitions. Interpreting these symbols is just like fortune telling. Once again, your mind interprets a sign it sees and links it to a belief hidden in your subconscious.

## Popular Divination Methods

Fortune telling is an ancient art. Countless archeological records of different divination methods were used in Ancient Egypt, Babylonia, and China as early as 4000 BC. Roman writers have also recorded the divinatory practices of the ancient Druids. While most divinatory practices were suppressed for centuries, they resurfaced in the 19th and 20th centuries and gained popularity again. Fortune-telling methods have come a long way, from entertaining parlor games to tools for gaining self-awareness and spiritual enlightenment. Below are several popular and simple divination methods you can try to learn more about your future, fortune, and superstitious associations.

# Scrying

Scrying is a technique that involves looking into a reflective surface and using it as a tool for gaining insight into different situations or finding lost items. Traditionally, scrying was done through a crystal ball or the moon. However, the practice has since evolved, and nowadays, you can use smoke, candle flame, a wood-burning fire, a large body of calm water (like a pond or lake), scrying bowls, small bowls with water, coffee grounds, and tea leaves. Not only that, but you can also use different pieces of nature or your environment to discern spiritual messages. Any object or living creature you see around you can be used as a scrying tool. In fact, most superstitions have originated from people's ideas when looking at a particular object or animal while scrying unconsciously. Besides answering simple questions, scrying can also help you find answers to tough questions and resolve challenging issues. You can find clarity in your relationships or learn about the consequences of your current actions. Or, you can scry to relax your mind and dissipate everyday worries. You only need your preferred scrying tool and relaxation techniques. Once you have those, you can start scrying.

**Instructions:**

1. Start by finding a quiet place where you won't be disturbed. Light a candle and turn off all the artificial lights and devices that might distract you. If you prefer, burn incense, put on some relaxing music, or use anything else you find helpful for relaxing. Your body should be upright, your shoulders relaxed but not slouching. Close your eyes and bring your focus to your breathing.

2. Set your scrying tool in front of you. Calm your mind and body until you reach a light trance-like state. Your mind should be focused solely on your intent. Some of the best ways to get into this state are mindfulness or breathing techniques, mantra repetition, and yoga.

3. When you've found the stillness within, you should now feel your senses radiating with spiritual energy and focus on your scrying tool.

4. Direct your gaze softly on your tool and keep an open mind to whatever thoughts or images the scrying tool inspires. You might not receive an answer to the question you've asked. If this happens, you were looking for something else deep in your subconscious, except you weren't consciously aware of it. Other times, the answer you get will be indirectly related to your question – you will just have to figure out how.

The key to mastering scrying is trusting your intuition. While this might sound pretty simple, it often requires a lot of practice, especially if you don't have experience using your intuition and divination tools. When you scry, you are communicating with your subconscious mind, asking for information stored there. This is beyond the reach of your conscious and your ordinary sense, so you aren't aware of them. Your subconscious will, however, project the messages onto the tool. They'll appear as images and thoughts you recognize, making your conscious mind aware of them. You'll need as much concentration as you can muster to do this. If you have trouble focusing, try practicing it late in the evening. At this time, you're less likely to be disturbed, and your mind will likely be less likely to get stuck on unrelated ideas.

You can still practice during the day if you don't have time or feel too tired to scry late at night. In fact, you can scry wherever you are doing something that requires you to stay still or focus on a specific task. For example, when you shower, you focus on taking a shower, and you're already shutting everything else out. Without realizing it, you're entering the trance-like state required for scrying. Because of this, moments like these are perfect for practicing scrying. Just look at the surfaces around you, and your intuition will come up with something.

# Tea-Leaf Reading

Tea leaf reading depicting a flying bird and a dog.
*https://commons.wikimedia.org/wiki/File:Tea_leaf_reading.jpg*

Tea-leaf reading, or tasseomancy, is a specific form of scrying. It is a relatively new method and has gained popularity in the past century. Like any other scrying technique, reading tea leaves requires you to use a surface to translate messages from your subconscious. You'll need teacups, a saucer or plate, and tea for tea leaf reading. When choosing your teacup, choose a rounded one with a shallow bowl and a large handle. It should be white or pale in color to create a bigger contrast between its surface and the tea leaves. This will make it easier to see the shapes and symbols and interpret their messages. When it comes to the brew, you'll need loose-leaf tea, and you can use herbal blends and blends with spices. The texture of the leaves should be medium, not too fine, but not too coarse either.

## Instructions:

1. Place a teaspoon of loose leaves into the cup and pour boiling water over them. Steep for 3-4 minutes. Alternatively, you can brew the tea in a teapot without a built-in strainer. The leaves will need to go into the cup along with the water. If you opt for this

method, stir the tea before pouring, so the leaves will be equally distributed in the brew.

2. After pouring the brew (or steeping the leaves in the cup), let the leaves settle a little more. When the tea has cooled to the temperature you like, take the cup with your non-dominant hand (use your left hand if you're right-handed and your right if you're left-handed).

3. Sip your tea slowly. Take your time enjoying it. This is crucial for relaxing before divination. Drink your tea in a calm environment. Turn off any device that might distract you, and take a few minutes to clear your mind.

4. As you sip your tea, start focusing on your intent. Do you have a specific question you want to be answered? If not, try to formulate one. Try aiming for a question that looks at the broader picture. For example, instead of asking: "What should I do tomorrow morning?" Try asking questions like: "Should I look for a job tomorrow morning?"

5. If you don't have a question, don't worry. For beginners, it's also acceptable to read tea leaves without questions. You'll get a general reading of your future, which is also great for practicing this divination method.

6. When only a tiny amount of liquid is left in the cup, swirl it in an anticlockwise direction. Repeat this motion two more times to spread the leaves around the sides of the cup.

7. Place a paper towel on the saucer and slowly turn the cup upside down, setting it on the saucer. Let the excess liquid drain out, tap the bottom of the cup three times, and turn it over.

8. Hold the cup by its side. Its handle should point towards your heart. Look at the contents of the cup from several angles. Study any symbols or particular shapes that catch your attention. Besides the images formed by the leaves, you should also look at the forms created by the white surfaces of the cup.

9. Take your time looking at how the shapes are formed. They might not look like anything, but don't discard any thoughts or images they remind you of. The images may not make sense to your conscious mind, but your intuition will find the hidden meanings. If you listen to it, it will translate these messages into your consciousness.

While there are no rules to tea leaf reading, there are a few things to remember. For example, the placement of the shapes can indicate specific areas of life. Shapes closer to cup handles are typically associated with family, home, and one's self-image. These areas might show you issues with which you are currently struggling. You should read the leaves in a clockwise direction, starting from the rim on the left of the handle. Going in a downward spiral, slowly turn the cup and continue observing the leaves until you reach the bottom.

Shapes near the cup's rim are linked to the immediate future. Whatever you see in them will be related to the next few days. Images in the middle of the cup correlate to events and situations that'll occur within a couple of weeks. The shapes at the bottom are associated with events due within the next month.

While there are symbol charts for tea leaves, the most effective way to get results is to listen to your intuitive meanings of the images. For example, if you can see a book in the images, this could be a message related to a new chapter in your life. Or, it could be associated with your love of reading, depending on what your gut tells you. While letters in the tea leaves are traditionally linked to important people in one's life, they could also relate to a place you want or will visit in the future. You should also pay attention to how the symbols are linked to each other. Some symbols have different meanings when they appear alongside others.

Firstly, you should only focus on deciphering messages from individual symbols. When you've mastered this, you can try to create a story from the different associations you discover in the tea leaves. According to lore, tea leaves can only uncover positive outcomes. Consequently, you should only focus on positive events and situations and avoid asking questions about the negative ones.

# Tarot Reading

**Tarot card reading.**
*https://unsplash.com/photos/D3SzBCAeMhQ?utm_source=unsplash&utm_medium=referral&utm_content=creditShareLink*

Tarot reading is a well-known divination method using Tarot cards with predetermined meanings and connecting them to one's subconscious. Each card has its own story, which is part of a much larger picture. To master tarot reading for divination, you'll need to learn about the primary meanings of the cards. Tarot decks consist of 78 cards, divided into the Major Arcana and the Minor Arcana. The 22 cards of the Major Arcana tell the story of a journey (commonly known as the Fool's journey). The 56 cards of the Minor Arcana display nuanced details of one's journey, situation, or outcomes. Tarot cards won't reveal exact scenarios from the future. However, they offer guidance for interpreting future events based on your thoughts, actions, and outside influences. Besides tapping into the general meaning of each card, Tarot reading also relies on your intuition. When looking at the cards you pull, you interpret them based on what your subconscious tells you about them. This encourages you to practice self-awareness and learn more about your deepest thoughts, desires, and needs.

## Instructions:

1. Prepare your body and mind by relaxing. After clearing your mind, start focusing on a question. Avoid asking questions that require passive answers. For example, instead of beginning your question with "Should I...," start with "What do I need to learn about..."

2. Try to ask a question that shows the broader picture, so the cards can illuminate a journey you need to take to reach the foreseen outcome. You can ask the cards why you're feeling anxious about superstitions. Or you can ask for guidance to understand your beliefs and inquire about what areas of life you should focus on to move past obstacles and superstitions.

3. Once you've thought of your questions (beginners should start practicing with just one), place the Tarot deck into your hands and shuffle it. You can use the overhead shuffle method and hold the deck in one hand and use the other to take cards from one place in the deck to another one. You can also cut the deck by dividing it into smaller piles, mixing the order of the piles, and combining them into one. Another way to shuffle is through the sweeping method. This involves laying out all the cards on the table, gathering them into a pile, and arranging them into a neat deck.

4. Pull a card from the deck. The easiest way to do this is to divide the deck on your left and draw the card from the top. You can also fan them out and pick the one you feel drawn to. The latter is particularly effective for connecting to your intuition.

5. As a beginner, start practicing with one card. Once you've learned how to interpret the messages of one card reading, you can venture into pulling several cards and doing popular spreads.

6. Once you've pulled a card, lay it face down. Take a deep breath and turn it over. Look at its imagery and words, and think about what they mean to you. Don't overthink it. Whatever thought comes to mind first comes from your conscious, and this is what you're looking for when using your intuition for Tarot readings.

7. If you can't find any meaning to the card you've pulled, refer to their predetermined symbolism. These can be great stepping stones for learning to decipher what the cards are trying to tell you.

One-card pulls are the easiest ways to get into Tarot readings. You can pull a card daily to strengthen your intuitive connection to the cards. They can answer simple questions, and if you're interested in getting more details, you can pull three cards. And when you're ready to do spreads, you can do a five-card layout for intuition and clarity or a seven-card reading for a more in-depth analysis of the different influences on your future outcomes.

# Automatic Writing

Automatic writing is another popular way of fortune-telling. Like Tarot cards, writing can also become a tool for extracting knowledge from your subconscious. Or you can use it to exchange messages with the spiritual world. You will only need a pen and paper and channel your intention to let messages flow through you without you consciously dictating this process. Alternatively, you can use modern writing methods (mobile devices, computer keyboards, etc.). Still, the traditional way is more likely to help you connect with your subconscious, and the more successful you will be in deciphering the future through automatic writing.

## Instructions:

1. Start by finding a quiet spot without distractions. Get a piece of paper and a pen or pencil, and remove any clutter from the space in front of you. Prepare yourself by meditating or doing any other mindfulness technique. The goal is to relax and start focusing on your intention.

2. When you've cleared your mind, think about the question you want to ask about the future. Try to formulate the inquiries as simply as you can. For starters, only focus on the most pressing question. You can address the question to yourself or a spiritual guide you want to contact.

3. Relax some more by taking a couple of deep breaths. When you're ready, put the pen into your hand. Let it touch the paper without consciously directing its movement. If you feel the need to control your writing, put the pen down and clear your mind before continuing.

4. Try not to consciously write but let your hand do whatever feels natural. Let it write automatically without looking at the paper. Close your eyes if it helps you avoid looking at whatever your hand is writing. Take your time. It might take a few minutes for the thoughts to start flowing from your subconscious.

5. When you've finished your session, look at the paper. At first, what you've written might not make sense, or your writing might look like you've scribbled random words, numbers, or pictures). However, you should still try to interpret it. Consider what each word or symbol means to you and what they might mean concerning your question.

6. If you haven't been able to decipher enough to answer your inquiry, don't worry. It sometimes takes a couple of attempts for beginners to get an answer to a question. Finding relaxation techniques that suit your personality often helps speed up the process. And when you start receiving messages, remember to be open-minded about them.

# Chapter 3: Looking for Signs and Omens in the Sky

In days of old, people believed the elements of the sky held indications and portents concerning their destiny. From the stars to birds' flights and clouds, within their imagination, there has always been a curiosity and excitement associated with divining one's fate via signs and omens in the sky. Ancient cultures embraced nature and looked to it for guidance and knowledge of things beyond human insight. As time has passed and we have developed an understanding of our physical world, these ancient beliefs have become something of a novelty or curiosity. Yet through all shifting perspectives of society, there continues to be fascination within every culture as to what is hidden in the blue expanse which towers above us each morning.

## What Are Omens?

Omens are signs or signals from the natural world that are believed by some to be indicators of future events. They can take a variety of forms, such as sounds, objects, or other physical things. Many cultures consider it to be a way of understanding the divine will of the gods and other supernatural forces. In some societies, omens are seen as good luck symbols; in others, they are more associated with fear and superstition.

Omens have been studied and documented extensively throughout human history. Ancient Chinese texts describe how omens were used to predict important events such as battles, floods, and weather patterns. The ancient Greeks also had a system for interpreting natural occurrences and seeing prophetic messages from the gods. In cultures around the world, birds have been associated with omens. In particular, seeing a white bird is said to bring good luck, while sighting a black bird is often seen as bad news.

In writing and literature, omens have long been incorporated into stories to create suspense or foreshadow upcoming events. Some examples include Shakespeare's Macbeth or Homer's Odyssey, where supernatural interventions act as warnings or portents of what is to come. Even today, some still believe that certain objects or occurrences can carry special meaning about their personal fate or fortune and use these as guidance for their decisions in life.

Overall, an omen is an occurrence or sign someone interprets as having a deeper spiritual meaning than how it may appear on the surface. According to different beliefs and traditions, it may bring either positive or negative outcomes depending on its form and context. Regardless of how it is interpreted, it reminds us that unseen powers beyond our control shape our lives.

# Good Omen vs. Bad Omens

Part of human culture for thousands of years, omens are believed to be signs from a higher power that foretell the future and can influence people's decisions and behavior. The idea behind omens is that they can provide insight into what is to come, and some people take them very seriously. There is a distinction between good and bad omens in many cultures, with the former being seen as favorable indicators and the latter as unfavorable.

Good omens often involve natural or supernatural events seen as positive or hopeful for the future. A rainbow could be seen as a sign of good luck or protection from danger, while sightings of certain animals, such as eagles, were considered auspicious events that would bring about success or fortune. Other examples include dragonflies, which signify change or transformation; ladybugs, which symbolize new beginnings; and four-leaf clovers, which are thought to bring good luck. These symbols all offer hope and promise a desirable outcome in whatever situation they appear in.

On the other hand, bad omens indicate undesirable outcomes and typically involve darker elements like death or misfortune. In some cultures, the appearance of certain animals, such as bats, was considered an omen of bad luck or death. The same was true of black cats crossing one's path. Other symbols, like a broken mirror, were also believed to bring about seven years' worth of bad luck, while sneezing three times was viewed as a warning of imminent danger ahead.

## What Could Have Influenced People's Beliefs?

Many believe these associations stem from ancient spiritual traditions that sought to make sense of the unknown by connecting them with known phenomena in nature. The fact that certain animals were rarer than others likely made them more mysterious and thus associated with greater power or significance in some cases. Likewise, colors such as those seen in rainbows had strong symbolic meanings since they could not be explained by natural means alone. People also attributed meaning to physical phenomena such as storms because they seemed so powerful and out of their control – something they attributed to divine intervention rather than just mere happenstance. Additionally, superstitions passed down through generations may have further solidified these beliefs. Regardless, it appears that humans will continue finding ways to interpret their environment and seek out meanings beyond what is tangible in this world.

## Mindfulness Exercise

Learning to understand the omens present in everyday life can be a helpful tool for staying focused on the present moment and noticing any signs or blessings in our lives. To begin, set aside some time each day to focus on small moments. This could be five minutes of positive affirmations, deep breathing exercises, or mindful meditation. This will help to clear your mind and leave you more open to receiving any messages conveyed through symbols and signs. As you go about your day, pay attention to coincidences, flashes of inspiration, and impressions that float into your mind. These insights could be hints about how to move forward with a complicated situation or offer insight into future possibilities. You should also learn to listen to both with your ears and heart. Consider all forms of communication as possible omens. Whether it is a meaningful conversation at the park or words on a billboard as you're driving by, it can help inform decisions and situations in life. Finally, make a note of how these signs are helping you notice subtle shifts within yourself to take action through any potential opportunities presented to you.

Mindfulness exercise to get and understand omens:

1. **Find a quiet space:** Start by finding a quiet place where you can be alone and undisturbed. It could be your bedroom, balcony, or even a park if you have access to one. Spend some undistracted time in this space and just focus on yourself being present.

2. **Take slow deep breaths:** Once you are in the right environment, take some slow deep breaths through your nose with your eyes closed. This will help clear away all the thoughts that may come up from the busyness of life or anxiety about what happens later on today or tomorrow. Focus only on breathing for at least five minutes, allowing yourself to relax and become more aware of the present moment.

3. **Become aware of your body:** After taking those deep breaths, start to become aware of your body and the sensations it is experiencing. Notice how your feet feel against the ground or if there is a breeze brushing against your skin. Pay attention to every detail you can sense at that moment without judgment or expectations. This will help bring you back into the present and allow you to be more attuned to potential omens around you.

4. **Open up to what's around you:** Now that you are connected with your own body, open up to what's around you. Take some time to observe everything that is happening in that environment, from people's conversations to birds flying nearby. Let your gaze linger on each thing without trying to analyze or understand it. Just observe from a distance and see what feelings you get from these things around you.

5. **Notice any meaningful signs:** After a few minutes of observing, start to pay attention to any meaningful signs that may appear. These could be anything from a bird chirping at an unexpected time to a sudden wind blowing through the trees. Tune into these moments and take mental notes of them to remember them later if necessary.

6. **Reflect on the possible interpretations:** After taking note of all the potential omens, sit back and reflect on what they could mean. Remember that omens are open to interpretation and have different meanings for different people. Don't be hard on yourself if you don't get clear answers immediately. Just take some time to

ponder the possible interpretations of these signs, and make sure you keep an open mind when doing so.

7. **Take action:** Once you have reflected on all the omens and their meanings, it's time to decide what you should do with this information. Depending on what type of omen it is, there may be an action or decision that needs to be taken for your life to move forward positively. Don't be afraid to take risks and trust your gut when it comes to making decisions, as these omens can often be a sign of something great that's about to come into your life.

By following this mindfulness exercise, you should be able to become more aware of the present and pick up any potential omens. Remember to keep an open mind when interpreting them, take action if necessary and stay focused on the here and now so that you don't miss out on any important signs or messages.

# Celestial Omens

## 1. Spotting a Shooting Star

Seeing a shooting star is thought to be an omen of good luck by cultures the world over. This superstition likely originated in the celebrations that used to occur when a bright "shooting star" was seen. Ancient Roman and Greek folklore linked stars with fate and fortune, so sighting one was often regarded as a sign that good luck was soon to come. In some cultures, it even symbolizes wishes being granted. Across cultures, seeing a shooting star is still widely viewed as a good omen and calls for hope, faith, and perseverance on our paths in life. No matter your background or beliefs, we can all bask in the beauty of watching a shooting star light up across the night sky and remember to keep our sense of wonderment alive.

## 2. Halo around the Moon

Seeing a halo around the moon has been an omen of bad weather for centuries, with tales about its meaning varying from culture to culture. The origins of this concept can be traced back to ancient Greece, where it was believed that Zeus, the chief god, would shoot arrows at the sky to produce rain or hail. Many cultures adopted this belief from there, seeing a lunar halo as a sign of Zeus' anger. Different cultures interpret its meaning differently; some say it foretells storms, while others believe it will bring luck and good fortune. However, what is widely accepted is that when a halo appears around the moon, there will be some kind of weather event coming in. Though science hasn't yet proved exactly what causes such halos to appear around the moon, one thing is certain: if you see one, you better get ready for something wild!

### 3. Spotting All Five Visible Planets

The inexplicable sight of all five visible planets in the sky at once is considered an omen across many cultures that spans generations and galaxies. An ethereal beauty, this rare occurrence is an indication of fortuitous events. The origins of this belief stem from ancient texts and cultures that incorporated astrology into their ways of living and mythologies from tales of folklore and civilizations from long ago, and people began to recognize how powerful figures in the sky could be to our lives. Believing in the cosmic power held within each planet's unique energy, stargazers have been drawn to the magnificent sign all five visible planets represent when they appear in a unified display. Aptly dubbed the Grand Conjunction, a special moment like this gives hope, signs of blessing, and faith that brighter times are ahead.

### 4. Seeing Sun and Moon Together

Seeing the sun and moon together in the sky has long been seen as a symbol of good fortune and wealth across many cultures and societies. Dating back to ancient times, such an occurrence was believed to have divine origins, with some believing it was an omen sent from the gods themselves. Some cultures viewed it as a sign that they would be blessed with abundant wealth, while others saw it as a warning against pride or overreach. In Chinese astrology, seeing a celestial body like the sun or moon during certain times of day was associated with change and comfort in life related to health, love, career, and other material concerns. In some tribal cultures, this alignment was seen as an opportunity for renewal and hope after a period of misfortune. The sight of the two combined can be quite awe-inspiring and spiritual for many people around the world. It is a personal decision whether it's something interpreted through sacred texts or taken more symbolically.

### 5. Lunar Eclipse

Seeing a lunar eclipse has a variety of meanings. For Hindus, such an event holds immense significance and is believed to be highly inauspicious. It is considered an omen of bad luck and a foreshadowing of poverty, death, or destruction. This view can be traced back to the ancient Hindu texts known as the Shastras, which attributed these ideas to lunar eclipses. Similarly, in Jewish culture, it represents the same spiritual and portentous meaning, as an eclipse symbolizes a sign from God. The idea of cosmic prophecy through eclipses is also found in some Native American tribes, who tend to view it as a means of prognostication. Overall, lunar eclipses are steeped in religious tradition and superstition used by many cultures worldwide to explain this rare phenomenon.

# Bird Omens

**Blackbirds symbolize the balance between nature and humankind.**

## 1. Birds Pooping on Your Head

While a bird pooping on your head might not seem like the most ideal way to receive good luck, it is indeed considered an auspicious sign across many cultures. Spanning Christianity to Hinduism, the notion that a dove leaving its droppings on someone's head symbolizes financial and material success has been pervasive for centuries. It also signifies fertility. The origins of this "good luck omen" is said to have begun when Noah released a dove after 40 days of rain, and the bird eventually returned with an unexpected, blessed surprise. People then assumed that if they were fortunate enough to be "blessed" by a dove in such a way, their fortunes would surely follow suit. Although it certainly doesn't make it any less gross when you are actually experiencing this unique event, perhaps thinking about the long-standing good luck tradition may help.

## 2. Blackbird Making a Nest in Your House

In many cultures, the superstitious notion of a blackbird making its nest in your home is considered a sign of good luck. It is believed that such an occurrence symbolizes the protection of one's house, joy, fertility, and prosperity for those living there. In Celtic tradition, a blackbird taking residence was taken as a sign from spirit guides or deities that peace and harmony would be brought to the home. It was also thought to bring luck in financial endeavors. Similarly, Native Americans viewed the nesting of a blackbird as a symbol of balance between nature and humankind and believed it to be an opportunity to forge a closer relationship with Mother Nature. In Norse culture, the nesting of this species of bird was considered sacred and symbolic of guidance in life paths if observed by humans. These are but some examples that point to the great cultural significance this omen has held throughout history.

## 3. Seeing Five Crows Together

Beliefs and superstitions about crows have been around for centuries, probably because they are incredibly intelligent birds. A popular omen has been that sickness will follow if you spot five crows, and *death will follow* if you see six crows. This may be seen as a grim omen, but it also can be interpreted as a warning for people to pay attention to their environment and the signs of nature that surround them. The birds' behavior may provide warnings or clues about the unspoken danger lurking in the air, whether it's an impending illness or some other tumultuous energy from elsewhere in the area, so that people take action to protect themselves and their loved ones. While this particular superstition seems morbid, it serves an important purpose in many cultures and doesn't necessarily mean one should live life in fear of crows!

## 4. Spotting an Owl During Day

Seeing an owl during the day is widely considered to be a sign of bad luck or ill portent, with a varied and, at times, contradictory meaning depending on the culture. In Ancient Roman folklore, an owl signified death and would scream when struck by lightning, while ancient Greeks associated it with fertility and wisdom. Some Native American cultures saw owls as war-associated symbols, while in Africa, owls were thought to signify witchcraft. This nocturnal creature is commonly seen as a symbol of darkness and misfortune throughout many cultures, despite its more positive connotations in some mythologies. The origin of such beliefs has been a source of fascination for historians. Some people believe that such superstitions are linked to early human tendencies towards animism, while others attribute it to the silent flight and nighttime habits of this solitary predator.

## 5. Tip Your Hat if You See a Magpie

Have you ever heard the phrase "Tip your hat to a magpie?" It is a phrase rooted in a superstition that originated centuries ago. The superstition goes like this: supposedly, if someone sees a lone magpie, they should acknowledge it by tipping their hat or bowing to prevent bad luck from befalling them. This tradition has been popular in many cultures, such as Indian, Irish, and British. Its origin is thought to come from folklore, which tells how magpies symbolize mysterious prophecies and wisdom. It is hard to know for certain where this superstition came from, but it serves as an interesting reminder of how past cultural beliefs seep into our everyday lives.

# Chapter 4: The Symbolism of Colors

Did you know that in some cultures, wearing a certain color on a specific day of the week is believed to bring good luck? For example, wearing yellow on a Monday in Thailand is believed to bring good fortune, while red is considered lucky on a Thursday in Mexico. Meanwhile, green is considered unlucky in some parts of India because it is associated with infidelity. In China, red is thought to bring good luck and is often used in celebrations like weddings and the Lunar New Year. Superstitions surrounding colors are everywhere, ranging from the common to the downright bizarre.

Colors can symbolize different things in different cultures.
*https://pixabay.com/images/id-2468874/*

But color superstitions aren't limited to clothing or personal items. In some cultures, even the colors of food have a significant meaning. For example, in Japan, eating black beans on the day of the Setsubun festival is believed to ward off evil spirits, while in many Western countries, eating black-eyed peas on New Year's Day is believed to bring good luck and prosperity for the year ahead. Whether you believe in the power of color superstitions or not, it's hard to deny their influence on our culture and traditions.

This chapter will explore the fascinating and often surprising world of color superstitions, from the common to the obscure, and discover how colors have shaped our beliefs and practices for centuries. So, let's take a journey through the rainbow and discover the intriguing and often amusing world of color superstitions.

# Red

In many Eastern cultures, red is associated with luck, happiness, and prosperity. For example, in China, red is often used during important celebrations, such as the Lunar New Year and weddings, to symbolize good fortune and happiness. Similarly, in India, red is often used in traditional clothing and is associated with love, passion, and purity. In Western cultures, however, red often has more negative connotations. It can be associated with danger, passion, and anger and sometimes symbolizes warning or prohibition. For example, red is often used in stop signs and traffic signals to signify danger or the need to halt.

Red is also associated with love and Valentine's Day, with many people sending red roses or gifting red heart-shaped items to their significant others. Interestingly, red has also been associated with political and revolutionary movements throughout history. In the 20th century, the color red was adopted by socialist and communist movements, such as the Soviet Union and the Chinese Communist Party, to represent the struggle of the working class and the ideals of communism.

**Superstitions:**
- In Chinese culture, red is believed to bring good luck and ward off evil spirits, especially during the Lunar New Year. It is common for people to wear red clothing, hang red decorations, and give red envelopes filled with money during the holiday. Red is also believed to bring success and happiness in other areas of life, such as in business or relationships.

- In some African cultures, red is believed to have healing properties and is associated with blood and vitality. For example, wearing red clothing can help improve blood circulation and promote good health. Red is also thought to protect against evil spirits and negative energy.
- In many Western cultures, seeing a red bird, such as a cardinal, is meant to be good luck or even be a sign from a loved one who has passed away. Some people believe their wish will come true if they make a wish when they see a red bird. This belief may stem from the idea that red is a powerful and auspicious color.
- In some parts of Europe, red is associated with witchcraft and the devil. Witches were believed to wear red to indicate their allegiance to the devil, and red candles were used in their spells. Some cultures also believe that red is a color of warning and danger.
- On the flip side, in some cultures, seeing a red object or animal is believed to be a warning of danger or an impending disaster. For example, in Russia, seeing a red sky at night is believed to be a sign of bad weather, while in some parts of Africa, a red moon is considered a bad omen.
- Red is also commonly associated with love and passion, and wearing red clothing or using red in home decor can enhance romantic relationships and attract love. Some people believe giving red roses or other red flowers to a loved one is a powerful symbol of love and affection.
- In India, people believe wearing a red bindi (a decorative dot) on the forehead can protect a woman and bring good luck. The bindi is often worn by married women and is believed to represent the third eye and the power of intuition.

# Green

Green has been associated with growth, renewal, and the natural world in many cultures throughout history. This association is likely since green is the color of plants and leaves, which are essential to life on Earth. In many cultures, green is seen as a symbol of new beginnings, regeneration, and hope. For example, in ancient Egyptian culture, the god Osiris was often depicted with green skin to symbolize his connection to rebirth and the life cycle. In Islamic culture, green is associated with paradise and is often used in architecture and design to represent new life and growth.

Green is also closely associated with the concept of fertility in terms of agriculture and human reproduction. In some cultures, green is considered to be a lucky color for weddings and is thought to bring good fortune to couples trying to conceive. Additionally, green is often associated with balance and harmony, perhaps because it is located in the middle of the visible color spectrum. In traditional Chinese medicine, for example, green is associated with the liver and is believed to promote balance and good health.

### Superstitions:

- In some parts of Europe, wearing green on stage is bad luck for performers. This belief may come from the idea that green is associated with fairies and other supernatural creatures, which were believed to interfere with human activity.

- In Irish folklore, green is associated with good luck and is believed to bring wealth and prosperity. The green shamrock is the national symbol of Ireland and is associated with St. Patrick's Day, celebrated on March 17th.

- In some Asian cultures, green is also associated with fertility and is believed to bring good luck to couples trying to conceive. For example, in traditional Chinese medicine, green is associated with the liver, which is thought to be the organ that governs reproduction. Green jade is often used in jewelry and other decorative objects to promote fertility and good luck.

- In some African cultures, green is associated with nature and is believed to have protective properties. It is often used in rituals and ceremonies to ward off evil spirits and promote good health and wellbeing.

# Blue

Blue is a color that is often associated with tranquility, wisdom, loyalty, spirituality, and masculinity. Across cultures, blue is frequently used to evoke a sense of calmness and peacefulness, such as the sky or the ocean. It is also associated with knowledge, intelligence, and wisdom, as well as with trust and loyalty in business and politics. Blue is also used in many religions to represent spiritual qualities, such as inner peace and devotion. Additionally, in some cultures, blue is associated with masculinity and strength, symbolizing qualities such as power and endurance. Overall, the color blue has diverse symbolic meanings that have persisted across cultures and time periods.

**Superstitions:**

- In many cultures, blue sapphires are thought to bring good luck and protect against harm. In medieval Europe, blue sapphires were believed to protect against poisoning and evil spirits, while in Hindu culture, they are associated with the planet Saturn and are believed to bring wisdom, clarity, and good fortune.
- **Blue Eye:** In some cultures, blue eyes are considered lucky or protective. For example, in Turkey and parts of the Middle East, it is believed that wearing a blue eye charm or "nazar" can protect against the "evil eye," a curse that is said to bring bad luck or harm.
- **Blue Flames**: In some cultures, blue flames are considered a bad omen associated with death and destruction. In Japan, blue flames are said to be the ghosts of the dead and are often seen at haunted locations. Similarly, in Hindu mythology, blue flames are thought to be the manifestation of the goddess Kali, who represents destruction and death.
- **Blue Butterflies:** In some Native American cultures, blue butterflies are considered a sign of good luck or a messenger from the spirit world. In Cherokee culture, blue butterflies are thought to bring messages of hope and guidance from ancestors or spirits. Similarly, in Chinese culture, blue butterflies are thought to symbolize love and joy and are often associated with the famous love story of the Butterfly Lovers.

# White

White is thought to symbolize purity, innocence, and spirituality across many cultures. In many Western cultures, white is associated with weddings, representing purity and new beginnings. In contrast, in many Eastern cultures, white is often connected with death and mourning, as it represents the end of life and the transition to the afterlife. White is also linked to cleanliness and sterility and is often used in medical and scientific settings. In some cultures, white is believed to have healing properties and is associated with spiritual purification and enlightenment. For example, in Hinduism, the color white is associated with the god

Vishnu and is used in religious ceremonies and rituals. Similarly, in Buddhism, white symbolizes the purity of the Buddha's teachings and is associated with inner peace and spiritual enlightenment. Overall, the color white holds a diverse range of symbolic meanings across different cultures.

**Superstitions:**

- **White Flowers:** In many Eastern cultures, giving someone white flowers, particularly white chrysanthemums, is considered to be a sign of bad luck and is associated with death and mourning. Similarly, some Western cultures often associate white lilies with funerals and are not given as gifts.

- **White Clothes:** In many cultures, wearing white clothes is believed to bring good luck and ward off evil spirits. In some parts of the world, white clothing is worn during religious ceremonies or rituals to represent purity and spiritual enlightenment. However, in some cultures, wearing white after Labor Day or before Memorial Day in the United States is considered bad luck.

- **White Animals:** In many cultures, white animals are considered to be sacred or special in some way. For example, in Hinduism, white cows are considered sacred and often worshiped. Similarly, in Native American cultures, white buffaloes symbolize peace and harmony, and their birth is seen as a sign of good fortune.

- **White Horses:** In some cultures, white horses are believed to be a sign of good luck and are associated with purity and spirituality. In Greek mythology, the god Apollo is often depicted riding a white horse, and in Hindu mythology, the god Vishnu is also often depicted riding a white horse.

- **White Owls:** In many cultures, white owls are associated with death and are believed to be harbingers of bad luck. In some Native American cultures, white owls are considered to be messengers of death, and their hooting is believed to signal the approach of a loved one's passing.

# Black

Black is a color that has been associated with a range of meanings and symbolism throughout history and across cultures. In many cultures, black is associated with death and mourning and is often worn at funerals and other solemn occasions. In some parts of the world, black is also linked with evil, darkness, and the unknown. However, in some cultures, black is connected with power, strength, and elegance. In fashion, black is often seen as a classic and sophisticated color and is often worn in formal or professional settings. In some cultures, black is also associated with wisdom, knowledge, and experience, as seen in the traditional black robes worn by scholars and judges. Overall, the symbolism of black is complex and multifaceted, and its meaning can vary widely depending on the context and culture in which it is used. While it is often associated with negative or ominous symbolism, it can also be associated with positive and powerful symbolism as well.

### Superstitions:

- **Black Cats**: In many cultures, black cats are associated with bad luck, witchcraft, and even death. It is believed that if a black cat crosses your path, it will bring you bad luck. In some cultures, however, black cats are seen as good luck, particularly in areas of England and Scotland.

- **Black Clothing:** In some cultures, wearing black clothing is associated with death and mourning and is often worn at funerals or other somber occasions. In other cultures, black clothing is associated with power and elegance and is often worn by wealthy or influential individuals.

- **Black Magic:** The term "black magic" is often used to describe dark or evil practices and is often associated with witchcraft, sorcery, and other supernatural practices. In some cultures, it is believed that black magic can bring about illness, misfortune, or even death.

- **Black Candles:** In some cultures, black candles are associated with negative or harmful energy and are often used in rituals or spells aimed at causing harm to others. In other cultures, black candles are associated with protection and the banishment of negative energy.

# Purple

Purple is often associated with luxury, royalty, and power. This association likely stems from the rarity and expense of the dyes used to produce purple in ancient times. For example, in ancient Rome, purple was reserved for the clothing of the emperor and the highest-ranking officials.

In addition to its association with power and status, purple is also sometimes associated with spirituality and mysticism. This is partly due to the fact that it is a less common color in nature and can be seen as otherworldly or ethereal. In some cultures, purple is also associated with creativity and artistic expression.

**Superstitions:**

- **Wearing Purple Clothing**: In some cultures, it is believed that wearing purple clothing can bring good luck or enhance psychic abilities. However, in other cultures, purple clothing is associated with mourning and is considered inappropriate for festive occasions.

- **Purple Flowers:** In some traditions, purple flowers are associated with spirituality and are often used in religious or ceremonial contexts. However, in other cultures, purple flowers are thought to bring bad luck or represent death and are avoided.

- **Purple Amethyst:** In some New Age and spiritual traditions, purple amethyst crystals have healing properties and can help enhance intuition and spiritual awareness.

- **Purple in Dreams:** In some dream interpretation traditions, purple is associated with wisdom, enlightenment, and spiritual growth. Seeing purple in a dream can be interpreted as a sign that the dreamer is on the right path and making progress toward their goals.

# Yellow

Yellow is a bright and dynamic color that has a wide range of symbolic meanings across different cultures. One of the most common associations with yellow is that of sunshine and warmth. Just as the sun is often associated with life, energy, and growth, yellow symbolizes happiness, joy, and positivity. In many cultures, yellow represents the dawn of a new day or the beginning of a new cycle of life.

In addition to its association with sunshine, yellow is also often connected with creativity and intelligence. Many cultures believe that yellow can stimulate the mind and enhance mental clarity and focus. This is why you might see yellow used in educational settings or in advertising for products that are meant to boost cognitive function.

## Superstitions:

- **Illness and Danger:** In many parts of Asia and Africa, yellow is associated with illness, danger, and death. Some cultures believe that wearing yellow clothes or using yellow objects can attract misfortune or bad luck.

- **Infidelity:** In Russia and some other Eastern European countries, giving someone yellow flowers is frowned upon because they are thought to represent infidelity. According to this superstition, yellow flowers are seen as a sign of betrayal, unfaithfulness, or disloyalty.

- **Good Luck:** Despite its negative connotations in some regions, yellow is also considered a lucky color in other cultures. In China, for example, yellow is associated with good fortune and is often used in decorations during the New Year.

- **Wealth and Prosperity:** In some parts of the world, such as Mexico and some African countries, yellow is associated with wealth and prosperity. Wearing yellow clothing or having yellow objects in the home is believed to bring good luck and financial success.

- **Spiritual Enlightenment:** In some spiritual traditions, such as Buddhism, yellow is seen as a symbol of wisdom, enlightenment, and insight. The color is thought to represent the light of the sun and the power of the intellect, making it an important symbol for spiritual seekers and teachers alike.

From the fiery passion of red to the lively excitement of yellow and from the soothing calm of blue to the purity of white, colors have held immense significance in cultures and societies worldwide for centuries. Superstitions associated with colors can be found in all corners of the world, and these beliefs often have deep roots in history and tradition. While some may dismiss superstitions about colors as irrational or unfounded, they continue to play an important role in shaping cultural practices and beliefs. Whether it's avoiding the color yellow in Russia or using red as a warning sign in Europe, colors have the power to evoke strong emotions and influence our thoughts and actions.

While it's sensible to approach superstitions with a critical eye, exploring the symbolism and beliefs associated with different colors can also be a fascinating way to learn about different cultures and their histories. Understanding the meanings and superstitions surrounding different colors can be a fun and enlightening experience.

# Chapter 5: Omens about Animals and Plants

Since the beginning of time, omens about animals, insects, and plants have fascinated and held a special place in the human imagination. People from all backgrounds and belief systems are intrigued by the idea that seemingly mundane occurrences can be interpreted to convey powerful messages about the future. In many cultures, one has only to look at an animal crossing its path to understand if good or bad luck is likely to follow. For example, in some places, people believe that seeing a lizard scurry across your way bodes ill for your upcoming journey while spotting a cricket could indicate good fortune on its way. Similarly, many societies see daunting warnings from certain plants. An oft-cited example is discovering a blooming yew tree near one's home, which soon foretells death in the family. The intertwining of superstition and admiration regarding omens about animals and plants has been a part of every culture throughout recorded history and continues to captivate our minds today.

## Omens about Animals

### 1. Cats

Cats have been linked to omens of all kinds. Cats can bring good or bad luck or both depending on the culture or circumstance! One example is the black cat superstition found in European folklore, which says that if a black cat crosses your path, it indicates an impending disaster. This belief originates in the Ancient Egyptians, who kept felines in their households as symbols of protection against evil forces, the opposite of what we believe about them today! However, some cultures view cats positively, such as the Japanese belief that a white cat brings longevity and good fortune. Whether a particular omen is positive or negative, one thing's for sure: cats sure make life more interesting!

## 2. Deer

Often viewed as a symbol of divine or spiritual power and knowledge, deer are powerful symbols in many cultures around the world. For instance, ancient Greek mythology has the story of the goddess Artemis and her relationships with deer. Artemis is associated with hunting, mysteries, and wild animals, being considered the protector of women in childbirth and an earthly embodiment of self-will. Interestingly, seeing a deer is considered a sign from Heavens that one should face their current problems gracefully and with dignity. This belief stretches across different cultures; however, it has its roots in Celtic lore which tells of a connection between the spirit world, humans, and nature, especially regarding sacred animals. Deer –gentle creatures by nature yet obviously strong enough to carry antlers for protection – became an example of being resilient regardless of hardships faced. However, some signs could point towards misfortune, such as if someone hears a roaring or bellowing sound from a stag, as this is thought to represent tragedy. Throughout different folklore, you can see how when faced with danger or fear, they often rely on stillness or running away rather than direct confrontation - two things we could all learn to do.

## 3. Dog

Omens and superstitions related to dogs are widespread in numerous cultures and have been for centuries. These omens and superstitions are often linked to these beloved animals' role in society. For example, in some Native American cultures, dreamcatchers were hung near areas where a dog might sleep or rest, as it was believed that dogs had the ability to influence dreams. Similarly, Chinese astrology considers dogs to be a symbol of loyalty and protection, with many families adopting a dog as a form of spiritual guardian. In Japanese folklore, seeing a black dog before starting an important endeavor is thought to bring good luck and success. On the flip side of this coin, there are also negative omens associated with dogs, such as when some believed that to hear hearing a dog bark on New Year's Eve could signal the death of someone within the house during the coming year. In Europe, it's taken as a bad omen if a dog crosses between two people– as it is thought that the couple will quarrel or, if they're engaged, their marriage will not happen. Some cultures around the world believe dogs can detect the presence of ghosts or supernatural forces. This can go back thousands of years, and one example is the Greek belief in Hecate, the goddess of terror and darkness. Even today, many people still adhere to these types of superstitions.

## 4. Fox

In Asian and Native American cultures, foxes are viewed as symbols of wisdom and cunning, while Europeans sometimes consider them more tricky and mischievous. One famous superstition about a fox is that the sighting of a red fox during the daytime is said to be an omen of ill fortune. It signifies bad news or an unexpected occurrence that could potentially lead to distress or misfortune. This belief dates back centuries, with some sources saying that it originated in Celtic folklore, while others link it to Chinese mythology and superstitions surrounding the legendary "nine-tailed fox" spirit. Additionally, some people believe that spotting a white fox at night is an omen of good luck or prosperity, so these omens can be good and bad, depending on the circumstances.

## 5. Rabbit

Rabbits have been associated with good luck, omens, and superstitions for centuries. In cultures worldwide, seeing a rabbit has always been considered auspicious. This is partly due to the animal's incredible reproductive rate. Rabbits reproduce easily and rapidly, making them a symbol of fertility and abundance. When you come across one in your path, it can indicate that happiness and fortune are coming your way. In many cultures like Korean, Vietnamese, and Native American belief systems, rabbits are also seen as having healing powers or compared to wise old grandmothers bringing positive energy into the home with their presence. Whether you see them as messengers of joy or spiritual healers, rabbits carry an unimaginable amount of power.

## 6. Snake

Over the centuries, snakes have been widely referenced in many cultures and religions. In various contexts, such as Christianity or Ancient Egypt, snakes have been seen as a positive or negative symbol of power, wisdom, and energy. The serpent is also thought to be an emblem of transformation. As far as superstitions go, some societies consider seeing a snake a lucky omen that may signify good fortune or success. On the other hand, other cultures believe that finding a snake will bring death and destruction, so it's natural to feel apprehensive when seeing one. Ultimately snakes are regarded as powerful symbols because they remind us of how powerful and instinctual we humans truly are and that, very much like the mysteries found in nature, we all possess an immense inner power that can be directed to something creative if properly managed.

# Omens about Insects

## 1. Ants

The belief that ants are a sign of good luck is a common superstition worldwide. In many cultures, having an ant nest near your home is seen as a harbinger of good fortune and success. It is believed that if an ant enters the house and follows you, it means that something positive will happen soon. It is also said that if you come across three ants traveling together in the same direction, this indicates luck and wealth will follow.

The flip side to this belief is that being bitten by an ant can have negative consequences. It is a sign that arguments or quarrels may soon arise in one's life. This superstition holds strong in some parts of Asia, where being bitten by an ant carries the belief that discord or disagreements will surely enter one's life.

Ants are revered for their hard work and perseverance, characteristics highly prized by many cultures across the globe, and so they have become symbols of strength, resourcefulness, and resilience. These qualities also mean that when an individual sees ants moving about their home, it can symbolize progress in whatever project or goal they are working on at the time. Additionally, due to their large numbers, ants have become symbols of fertility and abundance throughout history. Thus, their presence near one's humble abode could indicate good things to come from all corners of life, whether it be financial prosperity or more children added to the family.

## 2. Butterfly

One of the most well-known omens and superstitions regarding butterflies is that they are often seen as messengers from the beyond, more specifically from lost loved ones. It is believed that when a butterfly lands on someone, it could be a sign that this person's relatives or other loved ones will soon pay them a visit. In Greek mythology, for example, the butterfly was strongly associated with the goddess Psyche, known to represent the soul or essence of life. According to legend, if a butterfly landed on someone in ancient Greece, it would symbolize their soul being blessed by the gods above and that their family would soon be reunited. This belief also extended to Japan, where during times of mourning, it was said that when a butterfly alighted upon one's shoulder, it was a sign that their ancestor had visited them to express their condolences or offer comfort. Native Americans also saw butterflies as spiritual messengers from the heavens and often held rituals to honor this creature's connection with nature and those who had passed on before us. In some tribes, such as the Hopi, girls were given butterflies to wear in their hair at special ceremonies, which were said to help protect them against bad luck or harm. They also believed that if a white butterfly came into your life, you should expect an important message very soon.

### 3. Dragonfly

Ancient civilizations have believed dragonflies were prophetic, with some cultures believing that seeing a dragonfly was an omen of good luck or a warning about imminent danger. In many Native American tribes, the dragonfly symbolizes transformation and enlightenment because of its association with swiftness and inspiration. For this reason, it is seen as a source of hope to aid in overcoming obstacles. Dragonflies are seen as messengers from the spirit world, and they often signify change or transformation, either physical or spiritual. Seeing multiple dragonflies can mean you are being told to keep an open mind and remain curious; finding a dead one traditionally means someone close to you is deceiving you or has gone astray. One famous omen associated with dragonflies is that they are directly connected with the Fair Ones, also known as fairies or sidhe (pronounced Shee). In this belief, dragonflies can be seen as reminders that the spirits of Nature watch over us and continuously strive to be part of our lives. As messengers from beyond, the dragonfly symbolizes both spiritual and physical transformation. It, therefore, carries a message of personal growth and transformation if it lands upon you or your property. Dragonflies are thought to help bring about a balance between humans and nature by reminding us of our responsibilities toward keeping our planet healthy. Such messages encourage us to reconnect with nature and enjoy its beauty while being mindful of actions that can be detrimental. Bright-colored winged miracles and dragonflies will usually appear where there is water nearby, symbolizing abundance and hope for greater things to come.

## 4. Ladybug

Ladybugs are a beloved insect the world over, and their presence has been associated with luck and good fortune for centuries. In Asia, ladybugs were believed to signify an impending birth or an impending marriage. The Chinese believed that if a ladybug landed on a person's hand, it would bring them luck in love. In Europe, many cultures considered ladybugs to be harbingers of good luck as well. It was said that if one were to appear on your property, it could signify a prosperous harvest or success in business endeavors. In the UK and Ireland, spotting seven ladybugs together was said to bring seven years of happiness. In some cultures, such as Native American tribes in North America, dreams featuring ladybugs were thought to be prophetic messages from their ancestors. Ladybugs were also seen as omens of protection from harm and evil spirits in many cultures around the world. Some people even believed that having a ladybug near your home could prevent bad luck altogether.

## 5. Spiders

Spiders have been objects of superstition and omens for centuries. For example, some cultures view seeing a spider as an omen that you will soon be visited by a friend who will bring you good news or shared knowledge. This is the symbolism of the spider's web, which reminds us that we are all connected and share nature's wisdom. Spiders were also seen as sacred animals in ancient times associated with the Goddess Athena, the Greek goddess of Wisdom. Indeed, many people believe that spiders are messengers of good luck. So if you spot a spider on your travels, take notice and don't be afraid. It may just be bringing positive news for you, especially regarding hearing from an old companion very soon.

## 6. Wasps

Wasps have been regarded as signs of danger and jealousy in many cultures throughout history. In Ancient Greece, the Greeks saw wasps as an omen of envy, believing that if one encountered a wasp, it meant that someone was jealous of them. If a person sees multiple wasps flying around their home, it could mean they are being watched by jealous eyes or surrounded by enemies who wish to harm them.

In Japan, superstition surrounds the belief that when a wasp enters your home, it means bad luck is coming and should be quickly removed from the premises. The belief is so strong that some Japanese people will even go out of their way to avoid killing a wasp if spotted in hopes of avoiding any negative repercussions.

In Native American culture, wasps are seen as symbols of wisdom and protection. It is believed that if a person is being attacked or threatened by another person or animal, they may call upon the power of the Wasp spirit guide to intervene and protect them. Other cultures believe that seeing a wasp could also be an omen of warning, indicating possible danger ahead.

# Omens about Plants

## Foxglove

Foxglove plants can symbolize both good and bad omens.
https://pixabay.com/images/id-2372342/

In some cultures, foxglove plants are seen as being both good and bad omens. In some places, it is thought to bring luck and good health, while in other places, it can be thought to bring bad luck or even death. In Norse mythology, foxglove was said to have been used by Odin to scare away his enemies. He would wear a cape made of foxglove blooms while riding his eight-legged horse Sleipnir, across the night sky. This may explain why some people consider foxglove an omen of protection from danger or evil.

In Britain, there are several superstitions about foxgloves. One popular superstition is that if one were to walk around a ring of foxgloves three times, they would become invisible for a time. Another superstition is that carrying a piece of foxglove will make one immune from sickness or injury for a certain amount of time. It was also believed that carrying pieces of this plant with you when going into battle would protect you from harm and bring you victory in combat.

The Japanese also have their own beliefs about the foxglove plant. According to their folklore, stepping into a patch of the plant is believed to bring love and happiness in life. It is also said that if given as a gift, the giver will have luck in money and good fortune overall.

## Fennel

The use of fennel as a way to ward off evil and bring protection dates back centuries. In ancient Rome and Greece, it was believed that the herb had magical properties which could protect against malicious forces. It was used in religious ceremonies and worn around the neck to ward off the "evil eye." Similarly, in Medieval Europe and parts of Asia, people believed that fennel could be used to keep away witches, demons, spirits, and other malevolent forces.

In India, fennel has long been associated with protective powers as well. It is traditional for Hindus to hang garlands of fennel over doorways to keep out evil forces and promote good luck. It is also believed that burning or using essential fennel oil can help purify a space or person from negative energy. People often burn bundles of dried fennel while reciting prayers or mantras for extra protection.

Folk medicine traditions across the world have long used this powerful herb for medicinal purposes. In Scotland during the 16th century, children were given tea made with dried fennel seeds before bedtime to help ward off nightmares and bad dreams. Similarly, Native Americans considered the plant sacred and would place sprigs of it on their heads or clothing to protect them from danger while they traveled through unknown lands.

## Parsley

Parsley has a long history of being associated with superstitions and omens. It is believed that parsley was originally a gift from the devil himself. Some cultures think that the devil requires seven journeys between his realm and your garden before he will allow parsley to grow. Any seed that did not sprout was said to have been kept by him. This belief was so widespread that in 16th-century Europe, people would use their own blood as fertilizer for parsley to make it germinate more quickly.

This superstition has its roots deep in ancient European folklore and mythology. In Greco-Roman culture, parsley represented death and funerals due to its association with the Greek goddess Demeter's daughter, Persephone, who was kidnapped and taken to the underworld by Hades. Parsley also features heavily in many Christian rituals, where it is used as an offering or blessing during baptisms and other holy ceremonies. Parsley is also associated with love spells. A sprig of freshly picked parsley placed beneath one's pillow could allegedly bring good fortune in finding true love or help see into the future regarding relationships.

## Rowan Trees

**Rowan trees symbolize protection in Celtic Folklore.**

*Eeno11, CC BY-SA 3.0 <https://creativecommons.org/licenses/by-sa/3.0>, via Wikimedia Commons: https://commons.wikimedia.org/wiki/File:Rowan_tree_20081002b.jpg*

Rowan trees have long been associated with superstition and omens. In Celtic folklore, the rowan is a symbol of protection, as it has protective powers that ward off evil spirits and bad luck. The symbolism behind the tree dates back centuries to ancient European culture, where people believed that planting rowan trees around their homes would protect them from malevolent forces. In Norse mythology, Odin was said to have hung nine sacred rowan twigs in the heavens, which formed a magical protective barrier against dark forces. In Scottish Gaelic folklore, the rowans are known as "fid na ndruad," meaning "the tree of druids." Druids were said to perform rituals beneath the shade of these sacred trees, and they were used as a way to invoke protection and blessings upon those who sought them. Additionally, rowans were often planted near doorways in Scotland and Ireland to keep out bad luck or malicious intent.

In Eastern European cultures such as Poland, Lithuania, Bulgaria, and Romania, planting a rowan tree outside of one's home is believed to bring health and happiness into the household. It is also thought that carrying an amulet made from a piece of rowan wood can bestow one with courage and strength in times of need. In England during medieval times, people believed that if you crossed your fingers when touching a Rowan branch, you would be granted invisibility for a short time, allowing you to become invisible and be safe from harm or danger.

# Chapter 6: Lucky and Unlucky Numbers

Throughout history, humans have associated different meanings with different numbers. The concept of lucky and unlucky numbers has fascinated humans and has given birth to several cultural norms and practices. Let's explore these concepts in detail and determine how numbers influence our beliefs.

## Numbers and Superstition

Numbers have a long association with superstition, with people believing specific numbers have particular effects or special powers. Some link seeing or using these numbers with good luck and fortune, whereas others connect these numbers to bad omens. Let's read about superstition and numbers in detail:

### Lucky and Unlucky Numbers

Different cultures have particular numbers that are seen as lucky or unlucky. For example, in Western culture, the number seven is considered lucky because of the number's use in the Bible and the number's presence with cultural associations like the Seven Wonders of the World. The number seven also represents the colors of the rainbow. In contrast, 13 is considered unlucky because of its association with the Last Supper. This gruesome Biblical event records Judas Iscariot as the 13th guest, making the number seen as unlucky, especially from a religious perspective.

Likewise, in Asian cultures, the number eight is considered lucky because the sounds the number produces are similar to the word for prosperity. In contrast, the number four is considered unlucky because it sounds similar to death. These beliefs can often influence everything from business decisions to personal relationships.

## Numerology

Numerology is the study of numbers which allows exploration of the mystical properties behind numbers. People with a strong belief in numerology advocate that particular numbers can reveal valuable insights into a person's personality and destiny. For example, number one is linked with leadership, the ability to delegate, originality, and independence, whereas number nine is linked to humanitarianism, spiritual growth, selflessness, and care for others. Numerologists use several different methods to calculate a person's life path number. According to their beliefs, this path number contains all the information regarding the person's traits and life purpose.

## Astrology and Numerology

While numerology says numbers can reveal a lot about a person's destiny and life purpose, astrological studies advocate that the position of planets is a key influence on a person's destiny and life goals. For example, the position of planets in astrology determines the child's personality and destiny. Likewise, the numbers associated with a person's birth date can reveal their life goals and genuine personality. Here's an example from Western numerology. Specific numbers are associated with the letters of a person's name and added together to give a destiny number. This destiny number is believed to provide valuable insights into personality traits and reveal their strengths, weaknesses, and purpose.

## Numerical Coincidences

People who strongly believe in the effects of numbers see several numerical coincidences as a sign of good or bad luck. For example, seeing the same number throughout the day or period can indicate a good or bad omen. For example, seeing the number seven on the clock or license plates more than usual can mean good things are coming your way. Some even firmly believe that the number of letters in a person's name or the numerical values linked with each letter substantially impact a person's traits, personality, and life goals.

In a nutshell, the link between superstition and numbers is complex and deeply ingrained in many cultures. While these beliefs may not be based on scientific evidence, they remain essential in many people's lives and beliefs.

# Lucky Numbers

Lucky numbers are believed to bring good luck or fortune to those who use them. These numbers are based on cultural traditions, historical events associated with the number, or personal experiences. Many cultures have their own lucky numbers. While some cultures might see some numbers as lucky, other traditions can see the same number as drawing negative energies or indicating a bad omen. Below are some commonly used lucky numbers found in different cultures, beliefs, and traditions.

### Number Seven

This number is considered lucky in many cultures. Seven is often associated with good fortune, completion or fullness, and spirituality. This number is widely used in many religions, including Christianity, Islam, and Judaism. The association of seven in religious traditions symbolizes perfection and completeness.

### Number Eight

In Chinese tradition and culture, eight is considered the luckiest number. The sound the number eight produces when spoken in the Chinese language is similar to the sound of the word prosperity. Eight sounds like "Pa," whereas prosperity sounds like "Fa." This number is widely associated with wealth, success, and good fortune and is believed to have a pivotal role in business transactions.

### Number Nine

Nine is seen as a lucky number in Japanese culture. The number nine in Japanese has a similar pronunciation to the word "longevity." This association of similar-sounding words and numbers gives the number nine a special place in Japanese society. The number is linked to happiness, longevity, good health, and bliss.

### Number Three

Several cultures around the globe see the number three as a symbol of completeness, harmony, and unity. The number is widely expressed in art and literature and has a spiritual association.

# Unlucky Numbers

Unlucky numbers are believed to bring bad luck or misfortune to those who use them. These can be based on cultural superstitions or historical events and are often avoided or skipped altogether. Some of the most common unlucky numbers include:

**Four:** Considered unlucky in many East Asian cultures, four is often associated with death, as it sounds similar to the word for "death" in many East Asian languages. This number is often skipped or avoided in buildings, phone numbers, and other contexts.

**13:** Considered unlucky in many Western cultures, 13 is often associated with bad luck and superstition. This number is sometimes known as the "unlucky" or "superstitious" number and is often avoided or skipped in many contexts, including buildings and hotels.

**Six-six-six:** 666 is considered an unlucky number in many cultures, as it is often associated with evil or the devil. This number is sometimes known as the "number of the beast" and is often avoided or skipped in many contexts.

In addition to these typical examples, many other lucky and unlucky numbers vary widely from culture to culture. Some cultures have different lucky and unlucky numbers for different occasions or events. For example, in some Indian traditions, the number nine is considered lucky for weddings, while the number eight is considered unlucky for funerals.

Overall, lucky and unlucky numbers are a fascinating and complex part of human culture, demonstrating the deep connections between numbers, culture, and superstition. While these beliefs may not be based on scientific evidence, they remain essential in many people's lives and beliefs. They are a testament to the enduring power of human superstition and tradition.

# Folk Symbolism of Numbers

**One:** Unity, independence, individuality, beginnings, singularity. The number one is often associated with new beginnings and starting over. It represents independence and individuality, as it stands alone and is not divisible. It can also represent the singularity of the universe or a divine being. One can represent the self, leadership, confidence, and determination.

**Two:** Duality, balance, harmony, polarity, partnership, and opposition. The number two represents duality and polarity. It can represent the balance between opposing forces, such as light and dark, good and evil, or yin and yang. It also represents the concept of partnership and relationships. Two can represent harmony, cooperation, and diplomacy.

**Three:** Trinity, completion, perfection, spiritual awareness, creativity, and growth. The number three is often associated with completion, perfection, and the trinity in many religious contexts. It represents the unity of mind, body, and spirit. Three can represent creativity, growth, development, spiritual awareness, and connection.

**Four:** Stability, order, organization, the material world, the four elements, direction, and foundation. The number four represents stability and order in the material world. It represents the four elements (earth, air, fire, and water), the four seasons (spring, summer, fall, and winter), and the four directions (north, south, and east, west). Four can represent foundation, structure, and the importance of planning and organization.

**Five:** Adventure, change, flexibility, resourcefulness, versatility, and freedom. The number five represents change and transformation, the five senses, and the five fingers on a hand. It represents freedom, flexibility, and resourcefulness. Five can also represent adventure and the need for exploration.

**Six:** Harmony, balance, domesticity, family, community, love, and beauty. The number six represents harmony and balance in relationships, particularly in the context of family and community. It represents love, compassion, and empathy. Six can also represent beauty and aesthetics.

**Seven:** Mystery, intuition, spiritual awareness, analysis, wisdom, introspection. The number seven is often associated with mystery and spiritual awareness. It represents introspection, self-reflection, and the need for analysis and understanding. Seven is also associated with intuition and wisdom.

**Eight:** Abundance, success, infinity, material wealth, business, finances, power. The number eight is often associated with material wealth and success, particularly in the context of business and finances. It represents abundance, infinity, and the concept of power and control, and eight can also represent organization and management.

**Nine:** Enlightenment, completion, spirituality, universal love, humanitarianism, mysticism. The number nine represents completion and the end of a cycle. It is often associated with spiritual enlightenment and the concept of universal love. Nine can also represent humanitarianism and the need for compassion and empathy for others. It is associated with mysticism and the search for deeper meaning and understanding.

**Ten:** Completion, wholeness, achievement, accomplishment, integration, perfection. The number 10 represents completion and wholeness, particularly in achievement and accomplishment. It represents integrating and bringing together different parts to create a whole. Ten can also represent perfection and the search for excellence.

# Number Thirteen and Superstitions

The number 13 is one of Western culture's most well-known and enduring superstitions and is associated with various superstitions and folk beliefs.

One of the most common superstitions surrounding the number 13 is that it is considered to be unlucky. The origins of this belief are partially clear, but there are several popular theories about its origins.

One theory is that the superstition surrounding the number 13 can be traced back to the Last Supper, where there were 13 people present, Jesus and his 12 disciples, and one of the disciples, Judas, later betrayed Jesus. This has led some to associate the number 13 with betrayal and view it as a symbol of bad luck and evil.

Another theory is that the superstition surrounding the number 13 concerns the Knights Templar. According to legend, on Friday the 13th of October in 1307, King Philip IV of France ordered the arrest and execution of all the Knights Templar, a powerful and wealthy religious order at the time. This event has been associated with bad luck and misfortune and may have contributed to the superstition surrounding the number 13.

In Western culture, several popular superstitions and folk beliefs are associated with the number 13. Here are a few examples:

Triskaidekaphobia is the fear of the number 13 and is one of the most well-known superstitions surrounding the number. Some people are so afraid of the number 13 that they will go out of their way to avoid it by avoiding travel, signing contracts, or making major decisions on the 13th of the month or on Friday the 13th.

**Buildings without a 13th floor:** Many buildings and hotels skip the 13th floor altogether, labeling it the 14th floor instead. This is done to avoid the superstition surrounding the number 13 and make the building or hotel more appealing to those afraid of the number.

**Unlucky day**: In Western culture, Friday the 13th is often considered the unluckiest day of the year. Many people believe bad things are more likely to happen on this day and will take extra precautions to avoid accidents or misfortune.

**Unlucky in numerology**: In numerology, the number 13 is often considered unlucky because it is seen as a combination of the numbers 1 and 3, which are both associated with bad luck in some cultures.

**Lucky in some cultures**: While the number 13 is often considered unlucky in most Western cultures, it is actually considered lucky in some other cultures. For example, in Italy, the number 13 is associated with good luck and prosperity and is often used in the lottery and other games of chance.

Overall, the superstitions and folk beliefs surrounding the number 13 are complex and varied and demonstrate the enduring power of human belief and superstition. While these beliefs may not be based on scientific evidence, they continue to play an essential role in many people's lives and beliefs and are a testament to the deep connections between numbers, culture, and superstition.

# Spiritual Symbolism of Numbers

The spiritual symbolism behind numbers varies across different cultures and belief systems. In many spiritual traditions, numbers are believed to have deeper meanings beyond their mathematical value and are used to convey spiritual messages, truths, and wisdom. Here are a few examples:

**One:** In many spiritual traditions, number one represents the unity of all things and the universe's interconnectedness. It is seen as the source of all creation and represents the divine spark within each person.

**Two:** The number two represents duality and balance. It symbolizes the complementary forces of nature, such as yin and yang, light and dark, and masculine and feminine. In some spiritual traditions, the number two is also associated with partnership, cooperation, and harmony.

**Three:** Three is a powerful number in many spiritual traditions, representing balance and harmony. It is often seen as a trinity symbol, such as the Father, Son, and Holy Spirit in Christianity, or the three jewels of Buddhism (Buddha, Dharma, and Sangha). Three can also represent the past, present, and future, or the body, mind, and spirit.

**Four:** In many spiritual traditions, four represents stability and groundedness. It is associated with the four elements (earth, air, fire, and water), the four directions (north, south, east, and west), and the four seasons. In some spiritual traditions, four is also associated with materialism and the physical world.

**Five:** Five is often associated with the five senses, as well as the five elements (earth, air, fire, water, and ether or spirit). It is also seen as a symbol of balance, harmony, freedom, and adventure.

**Six:** Six is often associated with balance, harmony, and love. In some spiritual traditions, it represents the union of the divine masculine and feminine energies and symbolizes creativity and fertility.

**Seven:** Seven is a powerful number, representing spirituality, wisdom, and mystery. It is often associated with the seven chakras in Hinduism and Buddhism, the seven days of creation in Christianity, and the seven planets in ancient astrology.

**Eight:** In many spiritual traditions, eight is associated with abundance, prosperity, and success. It is often seen as a symbol of infinity and eternal life and is believed to bring good fortune and prosperity.

**Nine:** It is associated with spiritual enlightenment, transformation, and completion. It is seen as a symbol of the end of a cycle and the beginning of a new one and is believed to bring a sense of fulfillment and spiritual growth.

Overall, the spiritual symbolism behind numbers is complex and deeply rooted in many cultures and belief systems. While these beliefs may not be based on scientific evidence, they continue to provide meaning and guidance to many people on their spiritual journeys.

Beliefs about lucky and unlucky numbers vary greatly across cultures and regions, and what is considered lucky or unlucky in one culture may not be the same in another. That being said, here are some of the most commonly recognized lucky and unlucky numbers, along with associated superstitions:

# Lucky Numbers

**Seven:** Seven is widely regarded as a lucky number in many cultures and is often associated with spiritualism and mysticism. In some belief systems, seven represents completeness or perfection, as in the seven days of creation in Judeo-Christian tradition. Seven is believed to be a lucky number in China because its pronunciation is similar to the Chinese word for "togetherness" or "union."

**Eight:** In Chinese culture, the number eight is considered extremely lucky because it sounds similar to the Chinese word for "prosperity" or "wealth." As a result, the number eight is often associated with financial success and good fortune.

**Nine:** In some cultures, the number nine is considered lucky because it is associated with a long life. In Chinese culture, the number nine is associated with the Emperor and is believed to be the luckiest number.

# Unlucky Numbers

**Thirteen:** The number 13 is widely regarded as unlucky in Western cultures and is often associated with bad luck and even death. This superstition may have originated from the Christian belief that thirteen was unlucky because it was the number of people at the Last Supper (including Judas, who later betrayed Jesus).

**Four:** In many Asian cultures, the number four is considered extremely unlucky because its pronunciation is similar to the word for "death" in Chinese, Japanese, and Korean. As a result, many buildings in these cultures do not have four beliefs about lucky and unlucky numbers have been present in many cultures and traditions for centuries. These beliefs are often deeply rooted in superstition and not based on scientific evidence.

Lucky numbers vary from culture to culture. For instance, in Chinese culture, the number eight is considered lucky because its pronunciation sounds similar to the word for "wealth," while the number nine is considered lucky in Japan because it is associated with longevity. In Hinduism, the number 108 is considered very auspicious and sacred, while in the Western world, the number seven is often considered a lucky number, possibly because of its association with spiritual and mystical significance.

On the other hand, some numbers are considered unlucky in many cultures. The number 13 is the most well-known example of an unlucky number, especially in Western cultures. This is sometimes referred to as triskaidekaphobia. In many Asian cultures, the number four is unlucky because it sounds similar to "death." Similarly, the number nine is considered unlucky in Japan because it sounds similar to the word "suffering."

Superstitions associated with these numbers can range from avoiding using certain numbers or avoiding certain floors in buildings that contain those numbers to making important decisions based on a number's perceived luckiness or unluckiness. For example, some people may try to schedule important events on "lucky" days or avoid them on "unlucky" days, while others may avoid houses or buildings with certain numbers.

While these beliefs may not be based on scientific evidence, they continue to shape the way that people interact with the world around them, and the number four is often avoided at all costs.

**Nine:** While the number nine is considered lucky in some cultures, it is also considered unlucky in others. In Japan, the number nine is associated with suffering and misery and is often avoided. In Hinduism, the number nine is believed to be inauspicious because it is associated with the goddess Kali, often associated with death and destruction.

Overall, beliefs about lucky and unlucky numbers are deeply rooted in culture and tradition and can have a powerful impact on people's behavior and decision-making. While these beliefs may not be based on scientific evidence, they continue to shape the way that people interact with the world around them.

# Chapter 7: Superstitions about Food and Objects

You are at your friend's house, and it is raining hard outside. As you are about to leave, you open your umbrella before you go out of the door. Suddenly, your friend gasped and exclaimed, "What did you do?" There is a common superstition that it is bad luck to open an umbrella indoors, as people believe that it brings misfortune. There are many similar superstitions, like walking under a ladder, breaking a mirror, pouring salt, or cutting a banana will also bring you bad luck.

Similarly, many superstitions are associated with good luck, like hanging a horseshoe in your home or eating black-eyed peas. This chapter will cover the most common superstitions about objects and food and their history and origin.

## Food Superstitions

Every culture has its own food superstitions. Something acceptable in one country is considered bad luck in another. While some superstitions are related to history, others are derived from religious beliefs.

# Bananas

**Bananas symbolize freedom.**
*https://unsplash.com/photos/VI2rIoZUrks?utm_source=unsplash&utm_medium=referral&utm_content=creditShareLink*

Bananas symbolize freedom, abundance, and generosity. Cutting this fruit up is believed to bring misfortune; instead, you should break it into pieces. Banana peels should always be thrown in the garbage; if one throws them on the ground, they can experience a terrible fate. It is common knowledge that slipping on a banana peel can cause serious injuries, which is how the superstition originated.

Seamen consider bananas to be a bad omen, so you shouldn't take one when you are on a boat or ship.

## Black-Eyed Peas

Black-eyed peas symbolize good luck. Eating them on New Year's Eve in the USA will invite good health and prosperity into the coming year.

## Bread

Bread is considered sacred in many countries worldwide, with some cultures even treating bakers as priests. Almost everybody eats bread, so there are various superstitions related to it that stem from many regions.

## Baking Bread

According to a Scottish superstition, singing while baking bread is unlucky. Sometimes, after baking the bread, loaves get stuck together.

Count the stuck loves; if there are four, it means you or someone in your household will get married. However, if five loaves are stuck together, you will attend someone's funeral soon.

## Bread and Butter

Dropping a slice of bread and butter on the floor can have a meaning, depending on how it lands. If it lands on the butter side, this means that a family member or a friend is coming to visit you, so you should prepare your home to receive guests. However, others believe that if it lands on the butter side, you will experience bad luck.

It is inspired by a Latin superstition that says if a child's bread falls on the butter side, it is a bad omen, but if it falls on the other side, it is good luck.

This superstition influenced the saying "Why does bread always fall buttered side down?" which one says to indicate the misfortune that befalls them after the bread falls on the butter side.

## Cutting a Cross on the Bread

In medieval times, cutting crosses on loaves of bread could fend off evil spirits and protect you from witches. This superstition originated in England in the 1300s. A monk called St. Alban started this tradition and called it "Good Friday Buns."

Nowadays, in Britain, this superstition is still popular with people making bread and baked goods with crosses, but instead of making a cut on the bread, they draw it with frosting. Although people can make hot cross buns year-round, they are more common at Easter. In fact, people believed if you baked them on a Friday during Easter week, the bread would be enchanted.

## Cutting the Bread

The way you cut your bread can either bring you good luck or bad luck. Cutting a loaf of bread evenly will bring you good fortune, prosperity, and success. However, if the bread pieces turn out uneven, it means you are lying about something or keeping a secret.

In another superstition, ancient cultures believed that cutting bread with a knife would bring you bad luck. Bread is a gift sent from God, so you should break it with your hands, as using a knife is an insult to the Lord. However, if you must use a knife, don't cut it from both sides. Cutting the bread from one side will bring you prosperity and blessings.

### Finding a Corpse

Europeans and Indian Americans believed that one could use bread to find a drowned person. People would add quicksilver to bread, throw it in the water, and watch it float, and it would stop moving in the same spot where the dead body lay.

### Last Piece of Bread

Never eat the last piece of bread, even if you are starving, as it will bring you bad luck. If you are unmarried and eat the last piece of bread before someone offers it to you, you remain single forever.

However, if someone offers it to you with butter on it, accept it and eat it right away, as it will bring you good luck, love, or money.

### Making Your Mother-in-Law Love You

The Greeks believe that if you think your mother-in-law doesn't love you, eat the bottom part of a loaf of bread, and she will begin to like you.

### Placing Bread Upside Down

Placing bread upside down can bring misfortune and invite the devil into your home. This superstition dates back to fifteenth-century France. At the time, King Charles VII held many public executions. He would ask ordinary people to act as executioners – so anyone holding an ax could get the job done. Many Parisians felt uncomfortable around the executioners; some even hated them. Bakers expressed their feelings towards them by making low-quality bread for them. When Kings Charles VII found out, he ordered that bakers must treat all their customers the same, *including executioners.*

Bakers decided instead of having to deal with these men on a daily basis, they would bake high-quality baguettes and place them upside down. This indicated that the loaves of bread were reserved for the executioners, and no one was allowed to take them. Executioners would walk into the bakeries every morning, take the upside-down bread without talking to anyone, and leave.

Nowadays, people believe that placing loaves of bread upside down will invite an equivalent to the executioner, like the devil or evil, to your home.

### Rising Bread

If the bread rises while you are baking it, this indicates that a special person is thinking about you at this very moment.

## Throwing Away Bread

Throwing away stale bread is considered bad luck - and even *sin* in some cultures. If you drop bread crumbs on the floor, it can also bring you a lack of prosperity. In Russia, they believe that after you die, the bread you throw away will be weighed in the afterlife to determine if you will end up in heaven or hell.

## Throwing Bread in the Fire

According to ancient beliefs, if you throw pieces of bread into a fire, you will be feeding Lucifer. In another superstition, throwing it into a fire will lead to starvation. Ancient Catholics told children that Virgin Mary cried whenever they threw bread into a fire. For this reason, bakers cut a cross on the dough before placing it in the oven to protect it from the devil.

## Eggs

Eggs represent fertility, hope, the cycle of life, and purity. If you use eggs and find one with double yolks, someone in your household will have twins. This superstition originated in ancient Rome. However, in Norse mythology, an egg with two yolks foretells someone's death.

In Asian cultures, eggs are a symbol of prosperity and good fortune.

## Fish

Fish symbolize feelings, health, change, fertility, luck, and rebirth. In the Czech Republic, putting fish scales under your dinner dish on Christmas will bring you good fortune, and some people also put fish scales in their wallets to attract wealth.

## Garlic

Garlic is highly regarded in different cultures because it symbolizes good fortune and can protect against dark magic. In ancient Italy, people believed that if you ate a clove of garlic first thing in the morning, you would experience good luck. While in Greece, people believe that the word "garlic" signifies good fortune and that hanging a head of garlic in your home will bring you good luck and ward off evil spirits.

In Poland, adults would eat a clove of garlic and utter the word snake in front of children to protect them from any back luck that a snake can bring them. One of the most popular superstitions related to garlic is that it can protect against vampires.

# Grapes

**Grapes symbolize abundance.**

Grapes symbolize variations and abundance. In Spain and South America, people believe that eating twelve grapes at midnight on New Year's Eve will predict whether you will have a good or bad year. Each grape represents a month of the coming year. A sweet grape indicates you will have a good month, while a sour grape indicates bad luck will befall you on this specific month.

## Hot Peppers

If you are having a meal with a friend and they ask you to pass the hot peppers or jalapeños, place it on the table and ask them to pick it. Handing a friend hot peppers can cause trouble between the two of you.

## Noodles

In China, noodles represent long life. Cutting noodles while you are making them will shorten your life. Try to eat your noodles by slurping them to ensure you will live a long life.

## Onions

Onions are a symbol of unity, and in some cultures, they represent eternal life. It is believed that when you throw onion peels on the floor, you invite bad luck into your life and throw away good fortune. Hanging a small onion over your window will prevent evil spirits from entering your house.

### Rice

Rice symbolizes good health, fertility, success, wealth, and prosperity. You have probably noticed that people throw rice at weddings. This is an old tradition that originated in Italy, and it is believed to bring fertility and prosperity to newlyweds.

In the Philippines, eating rice from the bottom of the pot will lead to a series of losses in your life. For instance, you will be the last person to get promoted at work, lose a race, and be last in everything in life.

### Salt

Salt symbolizes preservation, purity, luxury, bad thoughts, and death. It is believed that spilling salt can bring you a string of bad luck. However, you can turn things around by throwing a small amount of salt over your left shoulder, as this is where the devil sits. This superstition originated from "The Last Supper Painting" by Leonardo da Vinci, where salt was spilled in front of Judas.

In ancient times, salt was very valuable and was used as currency. So when someone spilled it, they were wasting money, which is probably how it became a superstition.

### Yogurt

Yogurt symbolizes transformation and gratitude. In India, people eat yogurt with sugar before getting into a new business, and students eat it before an exam to bring success and good luck.

# Objects Superstitions

There are many fascinating superstitions from all over the world about different objects. Depending on your use, one object can bring both good and bad luck.

### Horseshoes

Horseshoes have always been a symbol of good luck. However, a few superstitions related to them show they are more than a lucky charm.

### Bad Luck

Hanging a horseshoe upside down can bring you misfortune, as luck will spill out. However, other superstitions say it can protect the house against the devil.

### Fending Off Evil

Hanging a horseshoe in your home will ward off evil spirits and invite good fortune. Good luck can also extend to anyone who enters your house. In some cultures, if you hang a horseshoe on your door and have a visitor, they should enter and exit from the same door, or they will take all the luck with them. This superstition dates back to ancient England when the Devil came to a blacksmith and asked to make him a pair of shoes. The blacksmith recognized him and nailed a horseshoe to one of its hooves. The devil was extremely distressed and in pain, and the blacksmith took advantage of the situation, tied him up, and imprisoned him. He agreed to release him on one condition: promise never to step into a home if a horseshoe hangs on the door.

### Under Your Pillow

On New Year's Eve, place a horseshoe under your pillow and sleep on it to invite good fortune into your life in the coming year.

### Ladders

Ladders symbolize ascension, progression, and the connection between the physical world and heaven. Many cultures believe that walking under a ladder can bring bad luck into your life. This superstition originated in ancient Egypt. The ancient Egyptians believed that the pyramids and all other triangular figures were sacred and powerful forces of nature, and it was unlucky to break one.

A wall and a leaning ladder would make a triangle shape, so when you walk under a ladder, you are breaking the triangle, which is a force of nature. The ancient Egyptians also buried ladders with their dead, so they could use them to ascend to heaven. They also believed you risk annoying and angering the gods and goddesses when walking under a ladder.

However, it wasn't until the Middle Ages that the fear of walking under ladders became common. A ladder leaning against a wall looks a lot like the gallows. During executions, the people who were getting hanged would only get to the rope by climbing on a ladder. Before executions, criminals must also walk under one. People believed that if one walked under a ladder, one would one-day face execution. This is why people associate it with bad luck and even death.

Another version of superstition is associated with religion. The Holy Ghost, the Son, and the Father represent the Holy Trinity and the number three, which is sacred in Christianity. Since a ladder leaning against a wall looks like a triangle, walking under one can break the sacred Trinity. It is also believed to be a blasphemous act, a sin, and can invite the devil into your life. When leaned against a wall, a ladder can represent a crucifix which symbolizes death and betrayal, so walking under it will bring bad fortune into your life.

## Mirrors

Mirrors are considered sacred in many cultures.
https://www.pexels.com/photo/oval-brown-framed-mirror-954539/

Mirrors symbolize vanity, arrogance, and water. In many cultures around the world, mirrors are considered enchanted and sacred.

## A Good Scare

Sometimes, you can get startled when you walk into a place and get caught off guard by your reflection in a mirror. Although this may feel embarrassing, it will bring you good luck. However, don't try to startle yourself on purpose because it will not be effective. The scare needs to occur naturally.

## Calming Your Nerves

Checking your reflection in the mirror when you are anxious or stressed will make you feel calmer and more relaxed. It is believed that the spirits will take all your problems away. However, looking in the mirror for a long time will provoke the spirits, and they can come for your soul.

## Bloody Mary, Bloody Mary, Bloody Mary

One of the most popular and creepiest superstitions associated with mirrors is *Bloody Mary*. According to legend, when you light a candle and dim the lights, say "Bloody Mary" three times in front of a mirror, Mary will appear to you as a reflection. She will scream or grab you by the throat. She can even escape from the mirror and chase after you.

This superstition originated in ancient England when the queen of England, Mary Tudor, gave orders to kill 280 Protestants.

## Covering the Mirror

Many people cover their mirrors after the death of a loved one. The belief is that spirits remain at their home until the body is buried. If the spirit sees a mirror, it will be trapped in it forever, and the mirror will take the person's appearance. This sounds like the plot of a scary movie.

Some people believe that mirrors are the devil's gateways and that they use them to enter this world. Covering the mirrors will protect you and your home from demons.

## Giving Mirrors as Gifts

In Asian cultures, giving newlyweds a mirror as a gift on their wedding day is bad luck. Mirrors are easily broken, and marriage should be strong and last forever, and they can be seen as a bad omen when you give them as a gift.

Mirrors can also attract evil spirits, so they aren't an appropriate gift to anyone, let alone newlyweds.

## Looking into the Mirror

If newlyweds look into a mirror together right after they get married, their souls will be united forever. They will also create an alternative reality where their souls will spend eternity together.

## Seven Years of Bad Luck

In ancient Rome, breaking a mirror will bring you seven years of bad luck. They believed that life renewed itself every seven years, which is when the curse would end.

On the other hand, a mirror that doesn't break no matter how many times you drop it symbolizes good luck. However, this doesn't mean you should keep dropping a mirror to get good luck because once it breaks, your luck will change for the worse.

## Umbrellas

Umbrellas symbolize femininity, shelter, power, prosperity, and protection. Many people worldwide believe that opening an umbrella indoors can bring them bad luck and unhappiness. The origin of this superstition goes back to ancient Egypt. The ancient Egyptians believed that opening umbrellas indoors was an offense to Ra, the god of the sun and the creator of the universe, so he was one of the most respected deities among his people. So when one offended him, they risked their anger and bad luck because they opened the umbrella away from the sun. Ra wouldn't just punish the person who opened the umbrella and all the people living in the house.

Some people believe that only a black umbrella or a new one will bring back luck if opened indoors. In modern times, people believe that opening an umbrella indoors isn't a good idea. It can invite ghosts and evil spirits into your home, bring discord between you and a loved one, and can also predict an impending death.

Superstitions about food and objects have been around for centuries. One object can bring both good luck and bad luck depending on the culture or how you use it. Some of these superstitions can even turn around the biggest disbelievers. For instance, eating a clove of garlic on an empty stomach doesn't only bring you good luck- it also prevents diseases. Opening an umbrella in your home won't only invite misfortune, but it can also damage your possessions.

# Chapter 8: Superstitions about Birth and Death

Superstitions aren't just related to numbers, animals, objects, or food. Many others are related to birth and death. Many old midwives' tales about pregnancy and babies have created fascinating superstitions that are popular to this day. Although various superstitions predict death, a few are related to burial, dead bodies, and cemeteries. While this can sound morbid, these superstitions have intriguing and interesting folklore tales associated with them.

This chapter will cover all the different superstitions about birth and death and their history and origins.

## Birth

Many birth superstitions from different cultures are related to childbirth, parenting, and child-rearing. Some can amaze you, others can scare you, and some can be strange. It is believed that many birth superstitions originated because of parents' confusion with childcare and giving birth.

### Announcements

In Bulgaria, women only share the news of their pregnancy with their partners and refrain from announcing the news to anyone else for as long as they can out of fear of the jinx.

## Blue Eyes

In Bulgaria, people believe bad luck will befall the child if someone with blue eyes looks at them. Getting rid of this curse would require the parents to wash the child's left foot and right eye twice a day for three days.

## Daggers and Scissors

In China, pregnant women shouldn't keep scissors, needles, or any sharp objects near their beds because they represent cutting the umbilical cord, which can lead to an early pregnancy or birth defects. However, they can keep a dagger under their beds because it protects the unborn child from evil spirits.

## Doctor Bear

There is a belief in Great Britain that if a baby sits on a bear's back, it will not get whooping cough.

## Eating Fish

In Canada, people believe that if an expectant mother craves fish, she should eat it immediately; her baby will have a fish head if she doesn't satisfy her craving!

## Eclipse

In India, it is unlucky for a pregnant woman to be exposed to an eclipse as it can cause deformities to the unborn child. During an eclipse, all windows and curtains should be closed to protect the pregnant mother from any rays of the eclipse.

## First Steps

In Bulgaria, parents have a lovely tradition called "Proshtapulnik" that they believe will determine their child's future. They set the table in their home and place a few items on it that are related to different professions. For instance, they can add a ball (sports), a ruler (engineers), a small board (teacher), and a toy stethoscope (doctors). When the baby takes their first steps and chooses one of these items, it will be their career when they grow up.

## Funerals

The Native Americans believed that expectant mothers should steer clear of funerals because this could lead to a miscarriage. They believed that pregnant women carrying a new life shouldn't be exposed to the end of life, as the unborn child will want to join the deceased and return to the spirit realm.

Jewish pregnant women also avoid funerals because they believe the deceased's spirit can get close to the unborn baby and cause them harm.

### Jump over the Baby

Catholicism is widespread in Spain, and many are devoted to their religious belief, so some of their superstitions are related to their faith. One of their popular religious festivals is called Corpus Christi and is celebrated in June, where they perform something called "devil jumping." In Catholicism, all babies are born with the original sin. So, they perform the Castrillo de Murcia tradition during the festival, which is meant to save the baby from this sin. Someone wears a yellow and red suit to look like the devil or El Colacho. Babies who were born in the last twelve months are put on mattresses in the streets then the devil character jumps over the babies.

Some Catholic churches believe that this jump purifies newborn babies from original sin. It will also prevent evil spirits from harming them and guarantee they lead a life away from the devil's influence. Just as with any superstition, some people are against this tradition and find that it can endanger the baby's life.

### Keep Babies Off the Ground

In Bali, Indonesia, newborns should be kept off the ground for about four months after they are born. Infants are sacred in Bali, so allowing them to touch the floor is considered blasphemy, as the earth can tarnish and ruin their pure souls. They are believed to be the divine spirits of their ancestors or reincarnations of their dead family members and should be treated with respect.

In Indonesian culture, the soul of a newborn baby isn't fully established yet, so if they touch the ground, this will interfere with the soul's development and its connection with the divine. Therefore, babies should be kept in their cribs. After three months, parents hold a ceremony for their toddler called "Nyabutan," where they cut the baby's hair, give them a name, and serve food to guests. They should also sprinkle holy water to appease the spirits. During this ceremony, infants are allowed to touch the ground for the first time.

### Leis and Pregnant Mothers

Leis are necklaces made of flowers, which tourists in Hawaii usually wear. Although it is a fun tradition, it can be bad luck for pregnant mothers to wear them. The Hawaiians believe that women who are expecting a child shouldn't wear leis or any type of necklace. Necklaces resemble the umbilical cord, so when a mother wears one, the umbilical cord gets tied around the baby's neck and ends their life.

In Hawaii, people also believe that Lake Waiau is enchanted, so throwing a child's umbilical cord in it will guarantee that they will live a very long life.

### No Celebrations

Nowadays, babies are celebrated before they are even born with ceremonies like baby showers or gender-reveal parties. However, in some places in Israel, these celebrations are frowned upon. Jewish families believe that any pre-birth festivities are unnecessary because you are celebrating an occasion that hasn't even happened yet, and you are rubbing your happiness in other people's faces which can invite evil and bad luck to the unborn child.

### No Mirrors

The Greeks believe that mirrors can seize a newborn's soul and trap it forever. For this reason, babies should never see their reflections. Some Greek families cover their mirrors with blankets when there is a newborn in the house.

Other countries around the world believe in this superstition. There are many superstitions around mirrors in different cultures because people always find them intriguing.

### Not Glowing

Pregnant mothers love it when people tell them they are glowing, except in Russia. Women there believe that these types of compliments are nothing but false flattery and can bring them evil and bad luck. If someone flatters a pregnant mother-to-be, she should wear a red thread as a bracelet for protection.

### Rubbing the Belly

Although many pregnant women enjoy rubbing their bellies to show affection to their unborn child, in China, it can lead to giving birth to a child who will be spoiled.

### Saliva

In the Philippines, various superstitions are derived from pagan traditions. People believe that babies experience something called *usog*, which is a feeling of distress that comes from being affected by an evil eye.

This usually happens when someone pays them a compliment. Because of this curse, the child could suffer from various diseases like a fever. Parents usually ask their friends and families not to compliment their babies. Suppose the baby is so cute that people feel the urge to praise them. In that case, they should say the incantation "pwera usog" to indicate that their words are well-intentioned and to protect the baby from distress.

However, if the baby is cursed by the evil eye, the person who cast the hex should rub their saliva on the baby's shoulder, forehead, and chest.

## Seven Days

In Egypt, families hold a traditional ceremony called "Sebou" seven days after the baby is born. It is similar to a baby shower with a celebration, food, and gifts for the newborn. During the ceremony, the baby is placed on a cloth on the ground, and the mother hops back and forth over them seven times. The purpose of this ceremony is to protect the child from evil. Salt is usually sprinkled on the new mother and all around the house to protect them from evil spirits.

## Sumo Wrestlers

No one wants to make a baby cry, but in Japan, it is encouraged as it brings the baby good luck. They even have a saying in the country: "Crying babies grow faster." There is a popular annual festival called *Nakizumo*, where sumo wrestlers try to make babies cry. Parents usually look forward to this ceremony as it determines their babies' health and future. The ones who cry the loudest will have the most blessings when they grow up because their cries fend off bad spirits.

## The Moon

There are many superstitions around a full moon, so it makes sense for pregnant women in some cultures to be wary of it. The Aztecs (an ancient culture in Mexico) believed that when a pregnant woman looked at the moon, her baby would be born with a cleft palate (a mouth deformity). When expectant mothers went out at night, they would wear something metallic to protect their eyes from the moon's rays.

## Touching the Belly

In many cultures, friends and families enjoy holding a pregnant woman's belly as it shows excitement for the new baby. However, in Liberia, pregnant women are very protective over their wombs. They believe that anyone touching it will invite evil spirits to kidnap the unborn child. They save this honor only for the people they trust, like family members and close friends.

### Ugly Baby

In Siberia, buying gifts for an unborn baby is considered an insult. After birth, people should also refrain from calling the baby cute or adorable and instead call them ugly because it brings them good luck.

### Wedding

In many cultures, it is a faux pas to try and outshine a bride on her special day, but it is a bigger deal in China. If a pregnant woman is in the same room with a bride and a groom, their fortunes will clash, resulting in bad luck that will only affect the unborn child.

### Death

Many people are terrified of death. Everyone knows they will die, but no one can ever know when or what will happen afterward. This mystery has led to many superstitions about death from different cultures worldwide.

### Clocks

Families in Europe stop all the clocks after a person dies.
*https://www.pexels.com/photo/wall-clock-at-5-50-707582/*

In many European countries, after a person dies, their family stops all the clocks at the time of death. This ancient tradition symbolizes that time has stopped for the deceased person. In modern times, this tradition is a sign of respect for the departed.

Not following this tradition will bring bad luck to the entire family.

---

## Day of the Dead

In Mexico, a famous festival called "The Day of the Dead" occurs on October 31st, the same day as Halloween. There are many superstitions surrounding this day dating back to Samhain and Paganism. Followers believe that on this day, the veil between the world of the dead and the world of the living is at its weakest, and the spirits of the dearly departed can cross over to the physical realm and visit their loved ones.

## East

There is a reason many graves are positioned to face the east, and it is related to religious beliefs. Christians and Jews believe that the dead will rise from the east on judgment day. However, this tradition predates both religions. Ancient Pagans, who worshiped the sun, believed that the East represented the future and the promise of a new life, while the West was associated with endings. They buried their dead east to west to symbolize living a full life, and just like the sun rises every day, they will also rise again.

## Feet First

In Victorian England, people removed the deceased's body from their home feet-first. This is meant to prevent the recently departed from looking back and invite someone else to join them in the afterlife. This is also why they used to cover the deceased eyelids with coins.

## Flowers

For centuries, people all over the world have placed flowers over the graves of their loved ones. However, some cultures have different interpretations of this tradition. The ancient Romans believed that the spirits of the dead roam around in graveyards. So, they would plant flowers there to create a nice space where their loved ones would spend their eternity.

In Europe in the 1700s and 1800s, people believed that flowers would blossom over the graves if a person led an honorable life. However, if weeds surrounded the burial grounds, they were bad and dishonest people.

## Gloves

Another superstition from the Victorian era is that pallbearers or anyone carrying a casket should wear gloves. People believed that the spirit of the dead could enter the bodies of the living through their hands and possess them.

During that time, people were preoccupied with death as there were many incurable diseases and resultant deaths. Christianity also teaches that the spirits leave the body after death. However, people at the time didn't know where the spirit went. They didn't know if the spirit stayed with the body or was free to possess others. Since people didn't have answers, they made up their own. This led to the belief that touching a casket can lead the spirit to possess you.

This superstition is still popular to this day.

### Headstones

Do you know that headstones originated from a superstition? Muslims, Christians, and Jews believe that when the world ends, the dead will rise and face judgment for their sins. This was a common belief among Europeans in the 1500s. However, they were worried that the dead would rise too soon. This is when they came up with headstones and placed them over the deceased head to prevent them from rising before their time came. In some places in England, they place the headstone at the feet so the deceased can't get up and walk.

### Healing Powers

In the US, people believe that dead bodies have healing powers. Standing next to one during a funeral can cure you of various diseases.

### Hearses

In the United States and many other countries, people believe that if a hearse stops in front of a house, someone in this house will die. In Africa, it is believed that three people from the deceased family will die if a hearse stops three times.

### New Shoes

In Victorian times, people refrained from wearing new clothes or shoes at a funeral as it showed disrespect and brought bad luck.

### The Philippines

Filipino culture has many fascinating superstitions about death.

- If you sneeze at a funeral, it is an invitation for the deceased's spirit to visit your home. However, you can uninvite them by asking someone to pinch them.
- Walking on guava leaves after a funeral will prevent the dead from following you.

---

- Never look at your house during a funeral, or you will bring more death and bad luck to your family.
- Don't go home after a funeral. Stop at any place first, like a coffee shop or a gas station, to prevent the spirit from following you home.
- Don't attend more than one funeral on the same day, or you or one of your family members will die next.
- Make sure that your tears don't fall on the casket, or the deceased cannot cross over to the other world.
- Whisper your wishes into the deceased ear so they carry them to heaven.
- Sweeping your home after the death of a loved one will banish their spirit and bring death to other family members.
- Break a plate after someone dies to stop the cycle of death.
- The spirits of the dead usually come back and roam around their homes. Family members should bury their loved ones without shoes to prevent hearing their footsteps.
- Adults should dress in black at funerals, but children should wear red so they don't get sick during the funeral or have nightmares afterward.

## Threes

You are probably familiar with this superstition; celebrities die in threes. For instance, David Bowie, Prince, and Alan Rickman all died in the first few months of 2016. The same happened with Michael Jackson, Farrah Fawcett, and Ed McMahon, who all died in June 2009. There are many more examples of three celebrities who died within days or weeks of each other. This superstition originated from old English folklore that three funerals took place within a short time frame.

## Thunder

In England, and specifically among Catholics, a thunderstorm after a funeral is believed to mean the deceased has entered heaven. However, if thunder hits during a funeral, this isn't a good sign as it means the departed will suffer in the afterlife.

## Tuck Your Thumbs

In Japan, you should always tuck your thumb when you walk near a cemetery. The thumb in Japanese is called the "parent finger," so by tucking your thumbs, you are protecting your loved ones. If you don't, you will bring death to one or both of your parents.

### Whistling

While it isn't appropriate to whistle at a cemetery, it can have more serious consequences. In America and Europe, it is believed that whistling at graveyards can summon demons.

### Yawning

Covering your mouth while yawning is more than just proper etiquette. This daily habit originated from superstition. At funerals during Victorian times, people put their hands on their mouths while yawning to prevent spirits from entering their bodies.

People from all over the world are fascinated with the magic of birth and the mystery of death. This has led to many superstitions related to the two. During ancient times, people didn't have the technology or science that exists today. They had to come up with their own answers for some of life and death's biggest questions. Many of these superstitions have lived on and are still practiced by many people to this day. There is a reason people still follow these superstitions in the modern world. They are harmless and can bring good luck and prevent misfortune. When protecting your unborn child and avoiding possession, it is better to be safe than sorry.

# Chapter 9: Wishes, Luck, and Fixing Bad Luck

This chapter sets out several superstitious activities to make sure luck will always follow you and your wishes come true. From carrying charms, such as a rabbit's foot, to knocking on wood or crossing fingers to blowing your birthday candle out, there are many ways to ensure your wishes come true. The chapter also lists several ways to fix bad luck if you've had the misfortune of inviting it unwittingly into your life.

## Luck-Bringing Superstitions

### Knocking on Wood

This saying is used in many cultures across the world. However, its origins can be traced back to the Celts, who believed spirits live in trees. According to the ancient Celts knocking on trees could call on good spirits for protection and eliminate evil spirits. Since many objects around the house were made from wood, the custom was subsequently transferred to these objects.

Christian beliefs are also linked to the power of wooden objects, such as the crucifix. This idea originates from Britain, just as the one attached to the 19th-century children's game "Tiggy Touchwood." This game is very similar to the modern tag game, except in this game, players tag one another by touching a wooden object.

### Blowing on a Fallen Eyelash

The tradition of blowing on a fallen eyelash comes from a 19th-century British folk tale. A person would place a fallen eyelash onto the back of their hand and toss it over their shoulder while making a wish. If the eyelash fell, their wish would be granted. However, their wish wouldn't come true if the eyelash stuck to their hand.

According to another version, the person should place the fallen eyelash on the tips of their nose, then try to blow it away. If they succeed, their wish will be granted.

There is also a belief that blowing on an eyelash can help you protect yourself from the devil or other evil influences. This idea comes from an ancient belief that the devil, evil spirits, and magicians collect human hair to gain power over people. Blowing away your eyelashes guarantees the devil can't get hold of it.

### Lucky Pennies

According to an ancient Romanian belief, finding a coin is a sign of good luck. This idea stems from a time when metal was considered highly valuable, so finding a piece brought many benefits to the finder. Other versions associate finding coins with the gods, referring to them as gifts and signs of protection. The person who found a coin was said to be favored by the gods and was under their protection.

The custom was carried into British, and later American, beliefs, where pennies took the role of luck bringing coins. Be careful when encountering a lucky coin. A penny will only bring luck if you find it facing up. If you find it tails up, turn it over rather than pick it up and leave it for the next person to find. Otherwise, it will bring you bad luck.

### Breaking a Wishbone

In Ancient Rome, the wishbone was seen as a symbol of luck. At first, it was discovering the wishbone during a feast that was considered lucky. Breaking the wishbone became a lucky tradition only after someone accidentally broke it while eating chicken. While breaking the chicken wishbone, the person coincidentally wished for something, and their wish came true. Nowadays, if you want to make your desires come true, you'll break the wishbone with someone else. As the bone snaps in two between your hands, the person who gets the longer piece of bone will have their wishes granted. If both parts are equal in length, both persons will have their wishes granted.

---

## Fingers Crossed

The superstition of crossing your fingers for good luck hails from Pagan beliefs common in pre-Christian Western Europe. Initially, the practice involved two people. A person made a cross with their own index finger and the index finger of another person. This was believed to combine their spiritual energies to ward off malicious spirits, get their wishes granted or seal a pact between the two.

Later, people realized they could invite their good luck by crossing the index fingers on their own two hands. Ultimately, the custom of crossing the middle and index fingers on one single hand was born, which is how the practice is performed today.

## Blowing Out a Birthday Candle

Blowing candles is related to an ancient superstition.
https://pixabay.com/images/id-1850982/

This custom is related to an ancient superstition that flames carry spiritual messages. In European folklore and magical practices, blowing a candle allowed the person to communicate with spiritual guides. According to the belief, if the candle flame is extinguished on the first try, the practitioner's message has been delivered. Similarly, if you blow out your birthday candles in one breath while making a silent wish, your wish will come true. However, it won't be granted if it takes several tries to blow out the candles or if you say the wish out loud.

## Tucking Thumbs Inside a Cemetery

In Japan, there is an ancient custom of tucking in one's thumbs when one visits the graves of their loved ones. This practice is linked to the

Japanese word for "thumb," which is also translated as "parent finger." The finger represents a parent or family member you must protect from death. You can keep your parents or family members safe from evil spirits by tucking your thumbs in when in a cemetery.

### Itchy Palms

In certain parts of Europe, and the Caribbean, an itchy right palm can indicate you're about to receive money. In contrast, if your left palm itches, it's a sign that you'll be out of money. These beliefs stem from the idea that a person's right hand holds active energy, which attracts money and good luck. While the left hand is said to carry passive energy, which deters money and good luck. In some cultures, the roles of the hands are reversed.

### Throwing Broken Dishes on New Year's Eve

In Denmark, people often save the dishes they have broken throughout the year, only to throw them at the side of someone's home on New Year's Eve. They usually bring the dishes to the homes of family and friends and hurl them at their homes, wishing good luck to the recipients in the coming year.

In a more subdued version of this practice, children in Germany leave a pile of broken dishes on the doorsteps of their family, friends, and neighbors. This way, they can convey their good wishes without potentially causing damage to people's homes.

### Sweeping Dirt Away from the Front Door

According to an ancient Chinese belief, good luck and benevolent spirits will enter your home through your front door. To ensure their homes will be blessed with good luck in the coming year, the Chinese sweep their homes by gathering dirt away from the front door. Sweeping dust away from the entrance also guarantees that none of the good luck that is already inside the home escapes when cleaning. If the collected debris is carried out from the house, it is done through the back door. They also avoid cleaning on the first two days of the New Year to prevent good luck from escaping.

### Bird Droppings

Strange as it sounds, in Russia, bird droppings are a sign of good fortune. You'll get money if bird droppings land on you, your vehicle, or your home. And if several birds leave their droppings on your property, you'll probably get a significant amount of money. You might receive a sizable inheritance or win the lottery.

### Spilling Water Behind Someone

According to Serbian folklore, spilling water behind a person's back is a sure way to bless them with good luck. It is believed that the fluidity of the moving water grants good luck to the person behind whom it lands when spilled. Serbians spill water behind friends and family facing challenging tasks, such as taking a test, traveling far away, heading for a job interview, etc.

### Eating Legumes on New Year

In Argentina, people seek to bring luck to their lives throughout the coming year by eating beans on New Year's Eve. Some Argentinians prefer to eat beans on New Year's Day to secure good luck, and it's also said to help keep their jobs. In Hungary, people eat lentils for similar purposes on New Year's Day. According to the Hungarians, lentils attract wealth; the more you eat on the first day of the year, the more money you'll have throughout the year.

### Accidentally Breaking Bottles

In Japan, accidentally breaking a bottle of alcohol is a sign of good luck. If you suddenly knock a bottle off the counter in a bar in Japan, people around you will cheer as they believe that you've invited good fortune to the place. On the other hand, breaking a bottle on purpose has the opposite effect.

### Planting a Tree

In Switzerland and some parts of the Netherlands, newlyweds often plant a pine tree outside their house to invite good luck to their new life together. Planting trees after a wedding is also believed to grant fertility. Others use trees or tree symbols in their wedding ceremony, seeking to bless their union and have good luck and fortune throughout their marriage.

# Fixing Bad Luck

## Using Salt

**Salt is believed to bring good luck.**

*https://unsplash.com/photos/4OlaTz6SdYs?utm_source=unsplash&utm_medium=referral&utm_content=creditShareLink*

Using salt is believed to bring good luck in many cultures. Interestingly enough, this belief originates from the same source that says spilling salt is a bad omen. Throwing salt over one's left shoulder is said to bring good luck because it chases away the devil who stands on that side. While it's most effective after spilling salt, throwing salt can also overturn fortune in other circumstances. However, throwing salt over one's right shoulder attracts more bad luck, which you don't want.

Alternatively, you can sprinkle salt into the corners of your home (or on the windowsill) to ward off bad luck. You can also cleanse yourself from negative energies by taking a saltwater bath.

### Handing a Broken Mirror

If you've broken a mirror and are worried about bad luck, be careful handling the pieces, as this will affect your fate. For example, throwing the pieces away seals the "Seven years of bad luck" curse. Instead, take the fragments and store them away until the next full moon. When it arrives, use a piece of the broken mirror to reflect the moon and gaze into the reflection. In many cultures and magical practices, it is believed that the moon can nullify bad energies. By staring into it through the mirror, you can reflect on the positive things in your life. When you're done, bury the mirror pieces.

## Using Incense or Herbs

In ancient herb lore, burning herbs is said to ward off negative influences responsible for bad luck. In modern times, you can achieve the same effects with incense, and this is especially true if you use an herb with an intense smell, like jasmine or sandalwood. If poor luck affects your personal life, burn incense at home by carrying it from one room to another.

Or, if you decide to go the traditional route, you can always burn sage. This herb has the most potent purifying effects and is guaranteed to help you turn your energies and luck around. Burning sage is also known as smudging, but you can use other herbs too. When you burn them, open your windows and doors so the negative energy can leave, and it will be replaced with a positive force and attract plenty of good luck.

## Carry Protective Charms

Protective charms are fantastic tools for warding off bad luck. You can carry them with you as you go about your daily life, and they will always protect you from negative influences. Even if you're already affected by bad luck, wearing a small charm on a chain or bracelet or carrying it around in a pocket can eliminate its effects. Here are some of the popular protective charms used by different cultures:

- **Four-leaved clover:** Wearing a charm in this shape is a great way to attract good luck. According to ancient lore, each leaf represents a lucky aspect of life, bringing love, wealth, health, and fame.
- **Keys:** Key charms have been used to invite good fortune since ancient times. To improve your chances of replacing poor luck with good, it's best to wear three keys, which will unlock the three doors of wealth, love, and health.
- **Horseshoe:** According to several ancient belief systems, horseshoe charms can ward off the "evil eye." Wear it on a chain with its ends pointed upwards. Otherwise, good luck will stay away from you.
- **Rabbit foot:** A rabbit's left hind foot is also believed to invite good fortune and wealth. Others suggest it can also protect you

from bad luck. You can also wear it on your key chain; you'll just have to remember to rub the charm regularly to activate its powers of bringing good luck.

- **Crystals and stones:** Their magical properties are used in different practices. Crystals and stones can provide protection and healing and bring positive energies. They're believed to have their own powers, which can amplify the ones in and near your body. You can wear them as charms or use them as decorations at home or at your workplace. Some of the most commonly recommended crystals for warding off bad luck are black tourmaline, labradorite, and amethyst. Rose quartz can help you replace the negative influences with positive energies and good luck.

### Engage in Charity

In many cultures, it is believed that the easiest way to invite good luck into your life is by doing good deeds. According to Buddhism and other Asian religions, you can repay any negative actions you have done by engaging in charitable pursuits. This is related to the concept of karma, which is a term these religions use for luck. Whether you donate to charity or help those in need in your environment, it doesn't matter. What matters is doing it altruistically and not just to earn good karma. Not to mention that engaging in charity can help you place things into a different perspective. What seems like poor luck to you can become a lesser issue when compared to the misfortunes other people face in their day-to-day lives.

### Unblocking Your Chakras

In many Asian cultures, the chakra system is connected not only to one's health but also to one's luck. By cleansing them, you can remove the block that hinders positive energy flow inside your body. You can purify your chakras with colorful flowers charged with the sun's positive energy. You can display the flowers on your table or use them in your bathwater to let them soak up the bad energy inside your body. Throwing the flower away afterward helps eliminate these influences symbolically.

### Encourage Spiritual Growth

If you're a spiritual seeker, you can also turn bad luck into good by promoting your own spiritual growth. You can do this by obtaining a level of spirituality that enables you to invite good fortune back into your life. In many religions, people pray to deities, spiritual animals, or ancestral spirits to improve their lives. While in other belief systems, gaining self-awareness is customary as part of a spiritually enlightening process.

If spiritual practices aren't for you, you can use self-reflection exercises and mindfulness techniques to learn which steps to take to better your luck. Positive affirmations and mantras can also help you invite good luck and chase away the bad ones. The more you repeat them, the more likely you'll be able to repel negative influences.

### Clean or Declutter Your Home

Decluttering or cleaning your home can help you eliminate negative energies that prevent the flow of good fortune. It's a simple practice that can empower you to make the change you need to fix your bad luck.

There are several beliefs attached to superstition. One of the most famous originates from South America, where people have a specific way of cleaning their homes. Young women need to learn how to clean their homes properly. Otherwise, they won't find a husband or will have bad luck even if they marry. To avoid this, they're encouraged to sweep when no one is around, so they can avoid going over anyone's feet with the broom, which is a bad omen. If one gets their feet swept over, they must spit on the broom to avoid misfortune.

In other cultures, it is believed the furniture in a home or workplace should be arranged in a certain way to encourage positive energy flow. To help this energy bring you more luck, clear away anything standing in its way, including unused items, cobwebs, and anything else that creates clutter.

Some also believe that the sun brings positive energy and good luck. This idea is associated with ancient beliefs revolving around sun deities who brought new life and fortune to people by reviving nature during spring. Even opening the window and letting sunshine surround your home can help improve your luck and fortune.

Alternatively, you can introduce bright light into your space by lighting large candles or having a wood-burning fireplace. The larger the area illuminated by the light sources, the less room there will be for bad luck to hide.

### Have a Change of Air

Traveling to another country is supposed to help dispel bad luck in many cultures. In ancient times, people often noticed that their poor luck stopped following them when they moved to another place. Or, even if they returned, the negative energies had dispersed, and their fortune turned for the better.

Nowadays, it's said that to get rid of bad luck, you must cross an ocean or travel to a country with different time zones. However, you don't necessarily have to go this far. Sometimes even leaving your home and workplace for a couple of days to take a trip on an extended weekend can do the trick. Sometimes all it needs is taking some time to understand what you need to change your luck.

## Avoiding Situations That Attract Bad Luck

Whether you're still fending off bad luck or don't want to attract it, aim to avoid behavior and circumstances that could invite misfortune into your life. Try to behave in a way that helps you avoid bad luck. For example, you can be extra careful not to break mirrors, walk under ladders, put your shoes on the table, "jinxing" yourself, step on a crack on the sidewalk, or open your umbrella indoors. Or in other words, you should avoid inviting other bad omens mentioned in the previous chapters.

It's also a good idea to familiarize yourself with some of the lesser-known superstitions (such as picking up a penny with the wrong side up) and other beliefs you might not be familiar with.

## Recognize the Signs of Good Luck

In many cultures, a small amount of good luck is believed to attract more good fortune. So, once you see the signs that your luck is turning from bad to good, try to pursue actions that can help you keep the positive flow going. Stay alert to recognize the signs and act in time.

# Glossary of Superstitions, Signs, and Omens

**1. Acorn**

It is believed that carrying an acorn in your pocket can bring good luck and protect against illness. Some people also believe placing an acorn on a windowsill can prevent lightning strikes.

**2. Apple**

If you cut an apple in half and count the number of seeds inside, that will tell you how many children you will have. Apples are also sometimes used in divination, where the way the apple core falls after it is cut can reveal information about the future.

**3. Bat**

Bats are seen as a sign of impending doom and are associated with vampires and other supernatural beings. In some traditions, it is believed that if a bat flies into your home, it is a sign that someone in the household will die.

**4. Black Cat**

Black cats are considered to be bad luck, and people believe they can cause illness or misfortune. Some believe that if a black cat crosses your path, it is a sign that you should turn back or change your plans.

## 5. Bluebird

It is said that if you see a bluebird, it is a sign of good luck and happiness. Some people also believe that if a bluebird flies into your home, it is a sign of good fortune and that you will soon receive good news.

## 6. Blue Moon

A blue moon is the second full moon in a calendar month, which occurs only once every few years. Some people believe that a blue moon is a powerful time for magic and manifestation and that wishes made under a blue moon are more likely to come true.

## 7. Broken Mirror

It is said that if you break a mirror, you will have seven years of bad luck, and some people believe that it can also release evil spirits into the world. To ward off bad luck after breaking a mirror, it's suggested that you bury the broken pieces in the ground.

## 8. Cherry Blossoms

Cherry blossoms are often associated with beauty and transience and are sometimes seen as a symbol of the fleeting nature of life. Some cultures believe if you see a cherry blossom in your dream, it is a sign of good luck and love.

## 9. Chinese Coins

In Feng Shui, Chinese coins are often used as a symbol of wealth and prosperity. It is believed that carrying Chinese coins in your wallet or purse can attract financial abundance and good fortune. Believers also suggest hanging Chinese coins on the doorknob of your home or office to invite prosperity into your life.

## 10. Chimney Sweep

In some traditions, encountering a chimney sweep is believed to be a sign of good luck. It is said that if you shake hands with a chimney sweep, or if a chimney sweep touches your shoulder, it will bring good fortune and ward off bad luck.

## 11. Clocks

In some cultures, giving a clock as a gift is considered bad luck, as it is believed to symbolize the ticking away of time and approaching death. Some people also believe that stopping a clock can bring bad luck.

## 12. Clover

The four-leaf clover is often seen as a symbol of good luck and is sometimes associated with St. Patrick's Day. Finding a four-leaf clover can bring good fortune, and carrying one in your pocket can attract wealth and success.

## 13. Crossed Knives

In some traditions, crossing two knives is considered bad luck, as it is believed to represent a potential conflict or argument. It is also said that if you accidentally cross your own knives while setting the table, you should quickly uncross them and make a wish to avoid bad luck.

## 14. Crossed Legs

Crossing your legs is sometimes seen as a sign of bad luck or disrespect, especially in certain cultures. In some traditions, it is believed that crossing your legs while sitting in a church or a temple brings bad luck and is disrespectful to the gods.

## 15. Crows on a Fence

In some cultures, seeing three crows sitting together on a fence is a sign of impending death or disaster. This superstition is sometimes referred to as "three on a match" and is thought to have originated from the belief that lighting three cigarettes from the same match was bad luck for soldiers during wartime.

## 16. Dandelion

In some cultures, blowing on a dandelion is believed to make a wish come true. It is also said that if you can blow off all the dandelion seeds with one breath, your wish will be granted.

## 17. Double Yolk Egg

Finding a double-yolked egg is considered a sign of good luck and prosperity. It is also sometimes seen as a sign of fertility and can be a good omen for those trying to conceive.

## 18. Dreamcatcher

Dreamcatchers are often used as a protective talisman to ward off bad dreams and nightmares. The dreamcatcher traps bad dreams in its web while allowing good dreams to pass through and reach the sleeper.

## 19. Eclipse

Eclipses have been seen as omens of change and transformation throughout history. Some cultures believe the appearance of a solar or lunar eclipse is a sign of impending disaster or war, while in others, it is seen as a symbol of good luck and renewal.

## 20. Friday the 13th

Friday the 13th is often seen as an unlucky day in Western cultures. Some people believe this superstition dates back to the Last Supper, where there were 13 people present, including Jesus and Judas. Others believe that it is related to the arrest and crucifixion of the Knights Templar on Friday the 13th in 1307.

## 21. Goldfish

Goldfish are often associated with good luck and prosperity. Some cultures believe that keeping goldfish in the home can bring good luck and positive energy.

## 22. Grasshopper

In some traditions, grasshoppers are seen as symbols of good luck and abundance. It is said that if a grasshopper lands on you, it is a sign of good luck and success.

## 23. Hamsa

The hamsa is a symbol of protection and good luck in many cultures. It is often used as a talisman to ward off the evil eye and negative energy. The hamsa is a hand-shaped symbol, with an eye in the center, and is often worn as jewelry or hung in the home.

## 24. Horseshoe

Horseshoes are often used as symbols of good luck and protection. It is believed that if a horseshoe is hung over a doorway with the ends pointing up, it will catch and hold good luck. If the horseshoe is hung with the ends pointing down, however, it is said that the luck will fall out.

## 25. Knocking on Wood

Knocking on wood is a superstitious act that is believed to ward off bad luck or jinxes. It is often done after making a statement of good luck or success in order to prevent anything negative from happening.

## 26. Ladder

In a lot of European cultures, walking under a ladder is considered to be bad luck. It is said to bring about misfortune and is to be avoided whenever possible.

## 27. Ladybug

Ladybugs are often seen as symbols of good luck and protection. It is believed that if a ladybug lands on you, it will bring you good luck and happiness. Ladybugs are also used as natural pest control, as they eat aphids and other harmful insects.

## 28. Leprechaun

In Irish folklore, leprechauns are mischievous fairies known for their elusive nature and ability to grant wishes. They are often associated with good luck and are said to have a pot of gold at the end of a rainbow.

## 29. Lightning

Lightning is often associated with danger and destruction. In many cultures, it is believed to be a sign of divine wrath or a warning of impending disaster.

## 30. Magpie

Magpies are often seen as symbols of good luck and protection, particularly in British and Irish folklore. If you see a magpie, you should salute it and say "Good morning, Mr. Magpie" to ward off bad luck.

## 31. Mirror Gazing

Looking into a mirror for an extended period is believed to bring bad luck or even summon spirits in several belief systems. It is also believed that breaking a mirror can bring seven years of bad luck.

## 32. New Moon

The new moon is often associated with new beginnings and fresh starts. In some cultures, it is believed that making a wish on the new moon will make it come true.

## 33. Pennies

Pennies are often associated with good luck and prosperity. In some cultures, it is believed that finding a penny on the ground is a sign of good luck and should be picked up and kept for good fortune.

## 34. Rabbit's Foot

In many cultures, a rabbit's foot is considered a good luck charm. Carrying a rabbit's foot is believed to bring good fortune and protect against bad luck.

## 35. Red Cardinal

A red cardinal is believed to be a messenger from a loved one who has passed away and is seen as a sign of good luck and a harbinger of positive things to come.

## 36. Red String

In some Eastern cultures, the red string is believed to have protective properties. It is often worn as a bracelet or necklace to ward off evil spirits and bring good luck.

## 37. Shooting Star

Many cultures believe that making a wish on a shooting star will make it come true. Shooting stars are seen as magical and rare and are often associated with good luck and positive change.

## 38. Silver

Silver is associated with purity and is believed to have protective properties. In many cultures, it is believed that wearing silver jewelry or carrying a silver object can ward off evil spirits and bring good luck.

## 39. Thirteen

In many cultures, the number 13 is considered unlucky. It is believed to bring bad luck, especially on Friday the 13th, which is considered an unlucky day in Western cultures.

## 40. Thunder

Thunder is believed to be a sign of anger from the gods or the spirits. It is often seen as an omen of bad luck, and some believe it is a warning of impending danger.

## 41. Toad

In some cultures, toads are associated with witchcraft and magic. It is often said that touching a toad can bring good luck or grant wishes.

## 42. Umbrella

In many cultures, it is believed that opening an umbrella indoors is bad luck. It is also said that leaving an umbrella open will bring bad luck to the entire house.

### 43. Vulture

Vultures are seen as symbols of death and decay. Seeing a vulture is often said to be a bad omen and a sign of impending danger or misfortune.

### 44. White Butterfly

Seeing a white butterfly is believed to bring good luck and is considered a positive omen. It is said that if a white butterfly lands on you, it is a sign of good luck and prosperity. And, if a white butterfly enters your home, it is a sign that someone who has passed away is watching over you.

### 45. Wishbone

It is believed that if two people pull on the wishbone of a turkey or chicken and it breaks evenly, both people will have their wishes come true. It is believed that the person who gets the larger piece of the wishbone will have good luck, and their wishes will be granted.

This chapter provides a helpful quick-glance guide to the many common superstitions people still believe in today. By understanding the origins and meanings of these superstitions, we gain insight into the cultural and psychological factors that continue to influence our beliefs and behaviors. While it is important to acknowledge the significance of superstitions in shaping our worldviews, it is also important to approach them with a critical eye. By separating fact from fiction and relying on evidence-based knowledge, you can avoid falling prey to superstitions that may lead us down harmful paths.

# Conclusion

This book has been a fascinating and thought-provoking journey exploring how superstitions have shaped our world and continue to influence our daily lives. From the common superstitions we all know to the lesser-known beliefs still prevalent in certain cultures, this book is a detailed look at the history and psychology behind these fascinating phenomena. Throughout its pages, you've explored the many reasons people believe in superstitions, from a need for control to a desire for comfort and protection. You now also know how superstitions have influenced everything from religion and culture to science and medicine.

As you reflect on what you have learned, remember that superstitions can have both positive and negative effects. While they may offer comfort and a sense of security, they can also lead to irrational thinking and harmful behaviors. It is up to us as individuals to approach them critically and question the validity of our beliefs. In the end, the power of superstitions lies in our ability to control our own thoughts and actions. By understanding the psychology behind superstitions, we can learn to recognize and challenge them when necessary and embrace them when they serve a positive purpose in our lives.

Superstitions are constantly evolving and changing over time. While some may have been popular in the past, they may not be as widely held today. Likewise, new superstitions emerge due to changing social and cultural contexts. Embracing the diversity of superstitions can be a creative and fun way to explore different cultures and perspectives. By learning about the superstitions of other cultures and communities, you can gain a deeper understanding of their worldviews and values and even incorporate some of these beliefs into your own lives. Whether carrying a lucky charm, avoiding certain colors or numbers, or performing a specific ritual, exploring superstitions can add fun and curiosity to your daily lives.

*"Superstition is foolish, childish, primitive, and irrational - but how much does it cost you to knock on wood?"* - Judith Viorst

This humorous quote by Judith Viorst highlights the contradictions and complexities of superstitions. While they may seem illogical or even silly at times, many of us still engage in them as a way to protect ourselves from harm or bring good luck. So, as you close the book on superstitions, maintain a balanced and curious perspective. While it's important to approach superstitions with a healthy dose of skepticism, acknowledge their emotional and cultural significance for people, and always be sensible.

# Part 2: Hekate

*The Ultimate Guide to Understanding the Goddess of Witchcraft and Ancient Greek Magic*

# Introduction

Whether you take an interest in the world of witchcraft or enjoy exploring the legends, mythologies, and stories of Ancient Greece, you've likely heard about the goddess Hekate. She has been a prominent figure in witchcraft for centuries due to her association with the underworld, crossroads, and the triple moon. Her stories feature her as a protector and guide, often portraying her doing magic and casting spells. Hekate, the guardian of the underworld, was believed to practice magic and perform rituals to guide and protect those journeying her territory.

Hekate also taught the goddesses Medea and Circe invaluable divination skills, such as the practice of herbal magic. This is why she is regarded as a symbol of guidance among the practitioners of magic. Wiccans hold Hekate in the highest regard, as they worship her as the deity of magic, darkness, and the moon.

This book serves as the ultimate guide to everything there is to know about Hekate as the goddess of witchcraft and ancient Greek magic. It delves deep into her attributes, mythos, powers, and archetypes and provides insight into how to safely work with her spiritually and ritualistically. Even though the book comprises comprehensive and historical accounts of the goddess, it's quite easy to understand and follow. This guide is suitable for those new to ancient Greek and witchcraft worlds and more seasoned readers alike.

By reading this book, you'll understand who Hekate really is, a multi-faceted deity who means different things to different people, and find out how she's regarded in the modern world. The book also explores the term

"Hekatean witch" and helps you determine how drawn you are to the deity and the best way to go about your practice. You'll learn about the various signs, tools, and symbols associated with the goddess and get to know the origins of the "Hekate's Wheel" or the Stropholos. You'll then find a practical exercise encouraging you to draw on your intuitive abilities to create a unique Hekate symbol.

You should be ready to initiate a connection with Hekate after reading the first few chapters, which is why chapter 4 serves as a step-by-step guide on how to make contact with the goddess. You'll find instructions and tips on performing certain meditations and visualizations that will help you access your intuition and a higher state of consciousness. The following chapter delves deep into Hekatean herblore and elaborates on the herbs most commonly associated with the deity.

This book also provides instructions on creating your own altar and adjusting it to appeal to Hekate. You'll find recommendations on which tools to incorporate into your shrine, guidance on consecrating and blessing them, and ideas on how to use them to strengthen your connection with the goddess. You'll understand how to make appropriate offerings and conduct various practical rituals. You'll also learn about the spells you can use to pray to Hekate and everything associated with her. Finally, you'll discover how to incorporate Hekatean magic into divination practices.

# Chapter 1: Who Is Hekate...Really?

Hekate or Hecate is a multi-faceted deity who means different things to different people. In ancient times, she was viewed as a three-formed (trimorphos), key-bearing (kleidouchos), and light/torch-bearing (phosphoros) goddess who resides on the roads and crossroads (einodia). She is associated with entranceways, night, light, liminal rites, and transitions.

**Hekate, or Hecate, is a multifaced deity in Greek mythology.**
*https://jenikirbyhistory.getarchive.net/amp/media/hekate-6e0c17*

Hekate is one of the most prominent deities in Greek mythology. She is portrayed as a "soteira," or savior of souls because she saved

Persephone, the goddess of Spring and the dead after Hades (god of the underworld) kidnaped her. According to the Chaldean Oracles, Hekate is also a world soul. Throughout history, her role has changed, with Medievalists and her worshipers limiting her role to only a goddess of witches and sorcery.

Nowadays, many women idolize her and view her as a feminist icon. However, she is often portrayed as a dark goddess or an entity that one can call upon for favors or vengeance. This is an unfair representation of what this powerful goddess truly represents. She can't be placed under one category since her personality has many different aspects; you'll discover those as you learn more about her.

So, who is Hekate, really? Is she good or evil? Is she a savior or a dark goddess? This chapter will uncover the mystery of Hekate and show you her true identity.

## The Name and Titles of Hekate

In Greek transliteration, Hekate is spelled Hekate, derived from the male name Hekatos, a term used to describe the sun god Apollo, meaning "the one who works from afar." However, no one knows the real origin of her name. In fact, some scholars argue that having a Greek name doesn't mean that she originated from ancient Greece, as some trace her roots to Caria in Asia Minor, which is located in modern-day Turkey.

In ancient Rome, Hekate was called Trivia, meaning "she of the triple road," representing her dominance over the crossroads.

She also has many titles attributed to her.

- **Nyktypolos:** Meaning "she who wanders at night," associated with her role as the goddess of witchcraft and magic
- **Chthoniē:** Meaning "chthonic," which symbolizes her role as the goddess of the underworld
- **Skylakagetis:** Meaning "leader of the dogs," which is also associated with her role as the goddess of witchcraft
- **Trioditis:** Meaning "she of the triple road," representing her role as the goddess of the underworld
- **Sōteira:** Meaning "savior," showcasing how she helps needy people

• **Other titles that reflect her good nature are:** "Kourotrophos," which means "nurse of the young," and "atalos," which means tender

## The Depiction of Hekate

In the very first depiction of Hekate, she was portrayed like any other goddess at the time, seated and wearing modest attire. Later, she was depicted in various sculptures as a female figure with three bodies and three heads to signify her role as the guardian of the crossroads, with each one of her sides guarding one of the roads.

## Hekate's Family

Hekate is the daughter of Asteria, the Titan goddess of nighttime divinations and falling stars; Perses, the Titan god of destruction; the granddaughter of Coeus, the Titan of intelligence; and Phoebe, the Titan of bright intellect and the moon. However, the Greek author Euripides believed that her mother was Leto, the goddess of motherhood. In other legends, she is portrayed as the daughter of Zeus, the chief deity and god of the sky, Demeter, the goddess of the harvest, or Zeus and Nyx, the goddess of the night. Others considered Hera, the goddess of women, to be her mother. However, it is believed that Hesiod portrayed the most accurate version of her heritage in his poem describing Asteria and Perses as her parents.

Her strongest association is with Demeter, who some often liken to Hekate. This close connection results from the close relationships both goddesses developed when Hekate helped Demeter find her daughter.

Although she is often portrayed as a virgin like Artemis and Athena, some legends state that she is the mother of the witch Medea, the monster Scylla, and other mythical creatures.

## Hekate throughout History

Anatolia (modern-day Turkey) was closely connected to Greece, and both countries experienced cultural exchange through migration, colonization, and trade. They also borrowed legends and deities from one another. It is believed that Hekate originated from Caria in Anatolia, and the ancient Greeks borrowed her and incorporated her into their pantheon of gods. Hekate had many followers in Caria, and she was the main deity in some towns.

The Greeks adopted Hekate into their mythology during the Archaic Period, where she underwent multiple transformations. Homer wasn't familiar with Hekate, so she didn't appear in Greek mythology until the Greek poet Hesiod first mentioned her in his poem Theogony. Hesiod didn't portray her as the goddess of the underworld or magic. However, he showed her as highly respected among the pantheon of the gods, with Zeus honoring and holding her in very high regard. In his poem, Hekate was the goddess of the sky, sea, and Earth, with no association with death or the underworld. She was a helpful goddess to the rich and poor, the weak and the strong.

In the fifth century, Hekate's portrayal was far from how Hesiod described her in early literature. She became known as a menacing and dark goddess. However, the Greek poet Pindar mentioned her soft side by describing her as "a friendly virgin." She was also accompanied by Erinyes or the Furies (deities of vengeance), who punished those who committed evil deeds. Her children, the Empusae (female demons), walked around seducing men.

Only in the fifth century did she begin having a more prominent role in Greek mythology. Before that, she played supporting roles in other goddesses' stories, like Artemis, the goddess of hunting and wild animals, Persephone, and Demeter.

To this day, she is still portrayed as the goddess of witchcraft and the underworld. However, no one knows why she has undergone this shift.

In the sixth century, Hekate was portrayed in a very different image. She was regarded as a cosmic soul or an entity that could be invoked by contemplating or practicing certain rituals.

No one knows when exactly people began to worship Hekate. Like many other Greek deities, she existed before written mythology. Ancient cultures passed down their stories orally from one generation to the next. Since there weren't source materials, these stories underwent many changes. People often added or omitted certain details until they differed from the original stories.

Although Hekate wasn't featured in Homer's epic poems, her daughter Circe did appear. In Odysseus, a sea witch called Circe plays a considerable role. Odysseus would seek her counsel so he and his men could safely cross the sea. She was described as an enchantress who could curse anyone who crossed her into beasts; she was also an expert in magic, just like her mother.

Hekate was featured in many works of literature as well. William Shakespeare mentioned her in association with strange rituals and dark magic.

# The Goddess

In Greek mythology, Hekate is the goddess of doorways, crossroads, magic, witchcraft, the Moon, agriculture, marriage, childbirth, ghosts, hellhounds, and other creatures of the night. She played a role in everything that concerned mankind, whether in life or death. However, Hekate was considered mainly a witchcraft and magic goddess during the fifth century. She is also associated with necromancy and the occult.

She greatly influences both the world of the living and the dead. Her dominion over necromancy and ghosts result from her ability to move between the realms. She also chooses the souls who can travel to and from the underworld, giving her the power to raise the dead and call on spirits. Whenever she roams the Earth, she is often accompanied by the souls of childless and unmarried women. Moving between different worlds was a recurring theme in Hekate's life since she was born in the realm of Titans, yet she found her place in the Olympian pantheon among the Greek gods.

She is a very powerful and mysterious goddess. One can't classify her as a good or evil goddess since she is capable of both. Some can flinch at the mention of her name, while others find her a safe haven that provides justice and protection.

However, this doesn't mean that Hekate should be feared. Her association with magic and witchcraft gives her the reputation of a sinister and terrifying goddess. The Greek author Hesiod, one of the first people to mention her in classical literature, described her as a kindhearted goddess who always provides help to those who call on her.

Hekate is also the goddess of boundaries like borders, city walls, or doorways. The most significant boundary in Greek mythology is the one between life and death. The ancient Greeks believed that the spirits of the dead crossed over this boundary to reach the other world. Hekate can be described as a veil separating both worlds while she stands guard in the middle watching over the living and the dead.

# Hekate and Witchcraft

The Romans and the Greeks worshiped Hekate as the goddess of witches. In the story of the Greek hero Jason and his heroic men, the Argonauts, who went on many adventures together, they sought the help of the witch Medea, one of Hekate's devotees and followers, to help them on their journey. The Hellenistic poet Theocritus also told the story of Simaetha, who invoked Hekate to bring back her lover Delphis.

Although Hekate is a protective deity and the goddess of boundaries, her most popular association is with magic. No one knows the origin of Hekate's transition to witchcraft, seeing as she first appeared as a kind goddess connected with light aspects. However, it is believed that she became associated with magic when her powers evolved, and she could grant favors to her followers. Being the goddess of all boundaries, including that between the supernatural and the natural, contributed to turning her into the goddess of witchcraft.

She became a dark witch due to her connection with the underworld. Since she could freely move between worlds, she could uncover secrets of the living and dead.

Hekate shared her knowledge of magic with her devoted followers like Medea.

# The Protector

Hekate is a protective goddess because of her role as the guardian of doorways and borders. She watches over cities and homes to prevent evil from passing through. She was often referred to as Apotropaia, which meant "to turn away," which symbolizes her role in protecting places. There is even a type of magic called apotropaic, inspired by the goddess, protecting homes from harm and evil. Even her dogs play a protective role. They acted as watchdogs by barking to warn homeowners of intruders or danger.

She doesn't just keep evil out, but she also allows it to pass through and enter homes. If you anger or disrespect the goddess, she allows bad luck and evil into their homes. Hesiod mentioned in his poem that Hekate had the power to allow or deny misfortune.

# Hekate Cults

The Greek geographer Pausanias stated that Hekate had many cults in her name on various Greek islands. For instance, a mysterious cult in Aegina worshiped the goddess and believed she could heal mental illness. In other islands like Miletos, Erythrai, Thessaly, Kos, and Samothrace, many cults were dedicated to Hekate, where her followers built altars and presented sacrifices in her honor. The goddess was also worshiped during the Roman and Hellenistic eras.

Hekate was worshiped in many other places worldwide, with various cults worshiping her privately or publicly.

# Hekate in Other Cultures

Hekate wasn't only popular among the Greeks and Romans, but many other ancient cultures called on her when they needed help with witchcraft. In ancient Egypt, a magical papyrus containing various spells and magical texts associated with Hekate was discovered. However, she was referred to by other names like Selene, Persephone, Brimo, and Baubo.

# Hekate in Greek Mythology

One can't truly know Hekate or her personality without learning about her roles in Greek myths.

### The Abduction of Persephone

Hades was in love with his beautiful niece Persephone. He knew her mother, Demeter was protective of her and would never give her hand in marriage to anyone. So, one day, he decided to kidnap her. As Persephone walked around the field smelling flowers, Hades climbed up from the underworld in a chariot and abducted her. Persephone was terrified and screaming, and the only one who heard her cry for help was Hekate.

After losing her daughter, Demeter was devastated and looked for her everywhere on Earth. Hekate came to her and explained that she heard Persephone screaming, but she didn't know who had taken her. Hekate suggested that Demeter would go to Helios (the sun god) to seek his help as he could see everything that happened on Earth. Helios told Demeter that Hades was the one who abducted her daughter.

Demeter was depressed and ignored her duties. As the goddess of agriculture, she abandoned the lands and crops, leaving mankind to starve. However, Hekate didn't leave her side and was her loyal companion until her daughter returned.

Zeus, Demeter's husband and Persephone's father, interfered and returned his daughter. Hekate was very happy to have Persephone back and to see her reunited with her mother. She became Persephone's attendant and accompanied her to the underworld. If it weren't for Hekate, Demeter would have never been able to find her daughter. She was also honored and highly respected in the cults of Persephone and Demeter for reuniting the mother and daughter. This incident also earned Hekate the epithet "sōteira."

## Zeus's Birth

Various myths tell the story of the birth of Zeus. In one version, Cronus (the god of time, king of the Titans, and Zeus's father) feared that his children would one day grow up and overthrow him. So, to protect himself, he swallowed them all after they were born. When his wife Rhea, the mother goddess, gave birth to their youngest, Zeus, she didn't want him to meet the same fate as her other children. She put a stone in clothes to resemble her newborn son and gave it to Hekate to bring to Cronus, who would swallow it instead of Zeus, who Rhea kept safe.

**Zeus**
https://pixabay.com/es/illustrations/zeus-mitolog%c3%ada-dios-griego-zeus-7683518/

This story shows Hekate as courageous, for who would dare to play a ruse on the king of Titans unless they were bold and fearless?

## The Attack on the Olympians

One day, the Giants attacked the Olympians (the main deities of the Greek pantheon). Hekate fought with the Olympians, and she managed to kill Clytius, one of the giants and the son of the Earth goddess Gaia. After helping the gods win the war, Hekate was highly revered by Zeus and all the other deities. Everyone saw her as a powerful goddess who they should never underestimate.

This shows Hekate as a brave and powerful warrior who would never shy away from a battle.

# Hekate in Modern Times

Nowadays, Hekate is mainly known as the dark goddess of witchcraft associated with ghosts. Although she doesn't make many appearances in modern Greek mythology, she plays a big role in Wicca, neopaganism, and modern witchcraft. The Triple Goddess, worshiped by many neopagans, is believed to be Hekate, who also has a triple form.

## The Contradictions and Mysteries of Hekate

It is believed that Hekate is the most misunderstood deity in Greek mythology – and this makes sense since she is the subject of many contradictions throughout history. She is portrayed as a guardian, protector of homes, and the goddess of witchcraft and the underworld. She can offer protection from harm yet allow evil and misfortune into people's lives. She is both a foreign and a Greek deity.

No one can understand the powers or origins of Hekate, especially since they underwent many changes in Greek mythology. Some scholars argue that Hekate is a different goddess than the one people are familiar with now. Since her name is derived from Apollo's other name, Hecatos, Hekate is believed to be another name for Artemis, Apollo's twin sister. As more and more people started to worship Artemis in ancient Greece, her followers noticed her many positive attributes. However, like any other deity, she has negative qualities as well. Her devotees separated the dark side of her personality to create a different goddess and gave her the name Hekate.

Although Hekate is known for being a witch associated with darkness and magic, many of her legends portray her positively, whether it was helping Demeter find Persephone or fighting alongside the Greek gods. On the other hand, some stories showed the goddess's dark side. In one story, there was a witch called Gale, who Hekate cursed and turned into a polecat because she found her behavior and desires unnatural.

Some scholars believe that Hekate is associated with the ancient Egyptian goddess of fertility Heqet who was linked to magic, which they called *heqa*.

Although various myths state that Hekate was the daughter of either gods or giants, some legends portray her as a mortal. According to some works of literature, she was a princess called Iphigenia who was about to die when Artemis saved her and transformed her into a goddess.

One can struggle to fully understand or define Hekate. She is one of few Greek deities who weren't featured in Homer's "The Iliad" or "The Odyssey," which is why little is known about her. However, she has appeared in various myths as the goddess of households, agriculture, witches, travel crossroads, and many others.

Hekate has always been surrounded by mystery, whether it's her origin or powers. She first appeared as the goddess of the sky with no association with witchcraft and - out of nowhere - her image changed as if she had become a different goddess.

Once again, we ask: who is Hekate, honestly? Is she a good or evil goddess? Answering this question isn't so simple. Every person has a definition of good and evil. Some would consider an action evil, while others may justify it. Hekate is just like human beings. She has positive and negative traits and is capable of wrongdoing. One can describe her as neutral. As the goddess of crossroads and boundaries, she stands between the living and the dead, and the natural and supernatural, so she is capable of good and evil.

In other words, she stands in a middle ground between two extremes, refusing to choose a side. You can choose how you want to view Hekate. However, one can argue that she is a feminist icon. She is portrayed in many of her legends as a strong, brave goddess who protects those who need her. Yet, she can't tolerate injustice or disrespect. She is an intriguing figure that you can't help but look up to and admire. Her kindness and darkness make her a goddess with human qualities that anyone can relate to her. The mystery and contradictions around Hekate are part of her appeal. She can pose more questions than answers, but her personality has two aspects, lightness and darkness, good and evil. Who Hekate really is can be open to many interpretations, with your personal view impacting how you see her.

# Chapter 2: The Hekatean Witch

Now that you've learned who Hekate is, you can delve into what a Hekatean witch is. This chapter provides recommendations on how to know you're drawn to Hekate and to what degree. You'll receive guidance on the broad range of ways the Hekatean witch works with the goddess, including the practice of finding one's own truth and receiving clarity when you're at a crossroads.

Being a Hekatean witch means following the path of the goddess.
https://unsplash.com/photos/43NPCi0NJlY

# Hallmarks of a Hekatean Witch

Being a Hekatean witch means claiming the path of following the goddess - on whatever journey she takes you on. Honoring her requires much work, as she is considered the Queen of witches. It includes venerating her regularly, invoking her for spiritual healing and assistance for growth, and building a connection with her. The Hekatean witch also honors all her fellow Hekate devotees - living or dead. In modern times, there is plenty of information available on the goddess. Unfortunately, some of it is rooted in misconceptions, which makes many curious spiritual and magical seekers hesitant to work with Hekate. A true devotee takes the time to delve into the ancient Greek lore of the goddess and the famous witches who venerated her. Through this pursuit, they understand how to reach out to the goddess and how she can help them.

As a Hekatean witch, you might also enjoy practicing her craft by reviving ancient Greek magic and incorporating it into your modern practices. A witch can choose many ways to venerate the goddess, including meditation, candle rituals, and herbalism. Many Hekatean witches are drawn to a natural lifestyle, preferring to use plants as natural remedies than treating conditions with modern medicine. They use various types and parts of herbs and ask Hekate for help when preparing them for treatments. Another characteristic of Hekatean devotees is a deep reverence for the balance of life and death. Instead of viewing death as the end of life, the devotees acknowledge death as a transitional period. Those crossing the liminal space must be honored through rituals and ceremonies. Dead ancestors gathered wisdom and passed it down to the new generations, for which they earned Hekate's respect. She helped them through their transitional periods, in life and in death. By celebrating the dead, you're honoring Hekate too. If you feel the need to honor your ancestors during transitional periods, it can be a great sign that you're ready to become a Hekatean witch. Liminal periods and spaces represent an in-between. For example, dusk is a liminal period between day and night. Samhain is a period dividing summer and winter. During these times, the divide between the world of the living and the spiritual realm is weaker, so it is natural to feel the pull towards the goddess and the dead souls she represents. You can feel drawn to family members, friends who've passed, or long-dead ancestors whose wisdom you can tap into during magical and spiritual practices. A witch will venerate all dead, make offerings, and ask for their blessing for magical work.

Hekate is known for her warm and kind nature - but she carries dark wisdom. True devotees understand that she has the power to cause harm. As long as you seek her out with the right intentions in mind, she will do you no harm. However, if your purpose is not pure, nothing good will come of working with her. For a Hekatean witch, the goddess represents the ultimate balance. They strive to obtain this balance by honoring the goddess through learning different practices.

The Hekatean witch knows that the goddess can only help those who wish to live a good life. Living one's life well means being aware of one's desires, strengths, and weaknesses. She can only help those who are helping themselves. She is there for those seeking their truth and wanting to find their authentic voices. True devotees will always make sure that their intentions are clear when calling on Hekate and take their time preparing for their magical or spiritual work. They know how crucial it is to be in a proper head space.

For a Hekatean witch, working with the goddess means seeking personal power. They know that the goddess won't do anything for them; they have to find their own power to overcome the challenges they face. At the same time, they never fail to show her humility. Hekate calls on her devotees to recognize the part of her that resides in all beings. She wants you to acknowledge that your soul comes from her essence. However, she also prompts you to find your own truths - your own spiritual path. As the goddess of balance, Hekate teaches you that there are times you need to be confident and stand up for yourself, establishing boundaries and stopping anyone who wishes to harm you. At other times, she will warn you to remain humble and look at challenges as opportunities for spiritual growth instead of insurmountable obstacles. If you feel that you should strive to be balanced like Hekate is, you're on the right path to becoming a true devotee.

A Hekatean witch seeks to celebrate and worship Hekate by being willing to put aside any prejudice, become her student, and accept her guidance. Many of her devotees express themselves through art and other creative endeavors. This allows them to connect with the goddess and draw on her powers to empower their practices. It allows them to obtain balance and resilience at the same time.

Devotees of Hekate are creative because her power guides them. They know how to express themselves through her symbols and many other spiritual and magical tools. They can find these everywhere. Staying true to one of Hekate's fundamental teachings, if you help yourself, she will be able to help you. For example, instead of using actual crossroads and liminal spaces, a Hekatean witch will create symbols of these from everyday items and situations.

Remember that all the above practices, beliefs, and pursuits are generalized descriptions of approaches used by Hekate devotees and priestesses. However, like any Hekate witch will tell you, working with the goddess is a highly personal process. Feel free to take inspiration from these practices and beliefs, but only embark on those that feel right for you. For your connection with the goddess to grow truly powerful, you must find your unique way of bonding with her and expressing your intentions and gratitude.

# Signs That Hekate Is Calling on You

The goddess is known for letting her presence known but is very careful about timing. A Hekatean witch knows that the goddess will only call on you when you need her and are ready for her help. You won't have to seek her out, nor does it do you any good to do so. As an ancient soul connected to all beings in the universe, she senses when she is needed. She knows when your life is thrown out of balance or when you're at a crossroads in life. If you are, she will come. If not, she won't help you. When she arrives, she will announce her presence with bold signs. She is an active deity - which is one of the main reasons she remains in the lives of her followers and is revered by many. Once you've established a connection with her and have begun nurturing your bond, she will keep reaching out to you. She will continue to guide you on your transitional journey as long as you need her.

According to certain beliefs, for Hekate to reach out to you, you must first ask for a sign from her. However, this isn't always the case. If you've never worked with her before, you can't ask for signs of her presence. However, she can present herself in symbolic messages. This is because, while you might remember asking her for help consciously, you might have actually done it intuitively. Intuition is a force with the power to make spiritual connections you aren't even aware of. To make sure that their goddess is contacting them, Hekatean witches often made offerings to ask if she was sending messages. They consider any signs they receive after completing the offering a confirmation.

The most common signs of Hekate reaching out to a witch or practitioner is seeing black or wild dogs. This might be a vision of a wild animal, like a coyote, feral dog, wolf, and fox. A black dog might even run up to you and try to make contact with you. If the dog's owner says that the animal rarely lets anyone pet them or go near them, this is a sure sign of Hekate inviting a witch on a journey. Hekatean witches also believe that hearing dogs barking (especially if the source is unknown) is also a sign of reaching out to them. It is believed that these are the sounds of deceased animals she used to communicate with her followers.

Seeing snakes is also a veritable sign of Hekate communicating with a devotee. These creatures are associated with magic, so if you have visions of them during your magical work, these might be messages from the goddess. Hekatean witches know that just as the goddess lives near the surface of the spiritual world, the snakes live near the surface of the ground. However, these animals tend to stay away from people, so there is typically a good reason for seeing them.

If you see keys, thresholds, doorways, torches, or lights, you're likely a Hekatean witch ready to embark on a long journey with the goddess. Finding old keys signals that you are about to cross a threshold that'll bring great changes into your life. Seeing how she is known as the light bearer, Hekate often communicates through light. In modern times, this will be through flickering streetlights and not torches. Still, if you see one flickering in multiples of three, you're about to receive a powerful message from Hekate.

Changes in temperature around you can also indicate that the goddess is near. Her world is a dark and cold place. You can feel when she reaches out to you from a liminal space by sensing a chill. You can also have a vision or dream in which the world around you becomes darker (even in the daytime) as if the sun has never fully risen.

# Be Careful When Working with Hekate

Hekatean witches believe their mistress isn't a deity to be taken lightly. She might not be the scary creature bringing death like some modern interpretations want to portray her, but this doesn't mean you can ask her for frivolous requests. She can help you transform your life - but only if you're truly ready to make meaningful changes. For instance, if your idea of transformation is landing a high-paying job, winning the lottery, or getting back with your ex, Hekate isn't the deity that can help you. While she won't retaliate for being asked these requests, you'll waste your time and resources because your work with her will be fruitless. On the other hand, if you wish to transform your life because you feel stuck or lost in a dark space, she might be able to guide you. It's all about wanting to find your own truth - and never about making or expecting miracles.

At this point, you might wonder how you'll know if you're ready for Hekate's help and how to ask her to find your truths. The first sign is your willingness to reach out and ask questions. It means you're aware that you're at a crossroads or in any other situation from which empowerment through Hekate can help you move forward. Next, you must accept that she is the goddess of change - not some dark witch who can retaliate if you don't act in a certain way. True spiritual conversions are rarely smooth. They're usually messy and painful. They require people to give up something, to leave comforting habits behind - and a true Hekaten witch knows and embraces this knowledge. If you reach out and your transformation begins, you must accept the pain that comes with it with humility. The witch never blames her mistress for the pain because she knows happiness can't be reached without it.

The next sign that you're ready for Hekate's help is that you're willing to open your mind to the messages you'll receive from her. Before you reach out, do a little introspection to see if you're ready for what it takes. Don't waste your time inviting Hekate into your space if you aren't. However, if you can adopt a mindset that welcomes transformation, you'll be good to go. This involves expressing gratitude for the blessing and lessons you've received so far, no matter how challenging the latter ones were. You can only move onto the next stage of life well lived if you already feel you've begun it. Affirmations about positive experiences and achievements often reassure you that you're doing good. The goddess is waiting for you to acknowledge that you're deserving. Once you do, she will send more signs and advice your way.

If you are ready to accept that Hekate will only be your guide while you do the hard work, you'll be even more empowered. Her power might be in you, but you control it, just as you control your emotions, thoughts, and actions. It's you who will be transforming your own life. The goddess will only assist you on your journey, occasionally steering you in the right direction if needed. You must accept responsibility and accountability for your actions and life. Your spiritual transformation will be your journey; you must gain self-awareness before it begins. You can't expect it to be easy, but you can help yourself by accepting it as a truth. With this approach, you'll be able to embrace the change, even if it comes in a way you've never expected it to arrive. This is what it means to speak your authentic voice. It's having faith in your power and not expecting someone else to do the work for you. Remember, she is all about telling as it is. She won't have anyone tell her she can't do something, nor should you.

Despite the painful changes that come with it, transformation can be beautiful. You'll know you're ready when you begin to act consciously. Instead of talking or daydreaming about changing your life, you're actually doing something that will start this process. This is when Hekate will step in. Because she won't help those who remain inactive, fearful of taking the first step, she will only guide those ready to move forward with their lives. She knows it's hard to leave the comfort and the known variables of your life behind - but she also knows it's necessary.

Some novices wonder whether Hekate will like them, often fearing that she will refuse their requests for assistance. When in fact, Hekate wants you to like yourself. She wants you to feel worthy of the positive transformation. You'll have no trouble communicating and bonding with her if you speak your mind and express your true desires. Hekate won't expect you to be perfect and not make any mistakes along your journey. After all, that's why she comes to your aid, to whisper her guidance as you work yourself through the messy and mistake-ridden transformation process. Hekate's authentic path is imperfect, *and this is what she is asking you to embrace.*

By embarking on her path, you've acknowledged that you'll accept any changes she brings. These will come in the form of spiritual messages, allowing you to know yourself better. You'll learn to identify your personal boundaries, a truly empowering effect of becoming a Hekatean devotee. You'll be able to say no when necessary – without justifying your words and actions. Hekate won't be responsible for this - you will. She will only push you to find your inner voice and the trigger you need to release it. Gaining self-awareness, self-confidence, and the ability to get in touch with your intuition even before you delve into in-depth work with the goddess are crucial achievements. They all signal you're ready to begin your journey as a Hekatean witch.

The last sign that you're ready to reach out to Hekate is that you accept that the goddess knows you better than you know yourself. You might be able to lie to yourself about wanting your life to go in a specific direction, but you won't be able to fool her. In these modern times, societal norms and financial obligations often create misleading desires. They can make you believe you can transform your life by having more money or becoming famous for the wrong reasons. However, the goddess knows that none of this is true, and you'll have to learn to listen to her.

If - after reading through all these signs - you still don't feel ready to start working with Hekate, don't worry. Take the time to learn what you truly want to do, and reach out to her when ready. She has been around for a long time and will continue to do so. She will wait for you until you're prepared to work with her. When *you do* start working with her, don't feel rushed to find your own truth. It's a long process that takes a lot of practice and intuitive work.

# How Strong Is Your Connection to Hekate?

Now that you know how the Hekatean witch follows her patroness and how to tell if the goddess is calling on you, you can learn more about how drawn you are to Hekate. The following quiz will help you glimpse at the level of your devotion and provide some pointers on how to go about your practice:

1. I feel drawn to Hekate during liminal periods, like when the day turns into the night at dusk or the summer transitions into winter during the fall.
2. I feel a deep desire to celebrate death as a transitional period knowing that life goes on beyond it.
3. I want to learn more about honoring Hekate and connecting with her.
4. I see signs of the goddess calling on me, sending me images of keys, black dogs, snakes, and death symbols.
5. I want to explore how to venerate Hekate through daily rituals.
6. I want to celebrate Hekate by visiting her temples and participating in rituals with other devotees.
7. I feel I am about to arrive at a crossroads, and Hekate can guide me through this transitional period.
8. I am ready to make changes in my life, accepting that if I ask Hekate for help, the changes will be powerful and perhaps painful.
9. Despite her might, I don't fear Hekate but revere her beauty and power, allowing her to guide me toward a better life.

## The Results

- You are simply curious if you've identified with only 1-3 of 9 statements. You've heard about Hekate and wish to explore more but aren't sure if following her is the right path for you. Continue your research to see if you can get inspired to forge your unique bond with the goddess and use her aid to transform your life.

- You are considered a true devotee if you've identified yourself with 4-6 out of 9 statements. You wish to honor Hekate and what she represents through regular practices. You're sure that she is the one who can help you live a better life, and you're ready to take on the challenges she brings forth to facilitate your transformation. Continue celebrating at her altar through small rituals fortifying your connection to her.

- If you've identified yourself with 7-9 of 9 statements - you are as devoted to Hekate as a priestess. You are ready to embrace the goddess in her every form and trust her implicitly. You accept that Hekate is everywhere and will know how to help when you need her assistance. You're inspired to devote a significant part of your life to Hekate and give into her transformative powers.

# Chapter 3: Hekate's Signs and Symbols

All gods and goddesses have signs and symbols associated with them. Often, these symbols are shown in illustrations or sculptures like the keys, dogs, and torches, usually depicted with Hekate. Since the goddess is associated with the night, many of her symbols are related to dark elements like the underworld and death. However, Hekate is also a mysterious goddess with many contradictions, so you will also find some symbols associated with light.

This chapter will cover all the different symbols of Hekate and their meanings.

## Hekate's Wheel

Hekate's wheel is also called the Strophalos of Hekate. It is a Wiccan symbol that belongs to the Dianic Traditions and Hellenic Recon. The wheel is a visual representation of Hekate. It consists of a six-sided star inside a circle surrounded by a labyrinth with three sides and another circle. The symbol first emerged in the first century when it was depicted with Hekate.

Hekate's Wheel.

However, some scholars believe these first images of the wheel were with Aphrodite, the goddess of love. Still, both images of the goddesses ended up overlapping.

Hekate is associated with the concept of the Trinity. She was first the goddess of the sea, sky, and earth. After she became associated with magic, she was depicted as a triple goddess with either three heads and one body, three bodies and one head, or three heads and three bodies. She is also associated with the three aspects of women's lives the maiden, mother, and crone. Hekate is usually referred to as the "Triple Moon Goddess" because she also represents the three different phases of the moon. The aspect of the trinity is a part of Hekate's identity, and it is apparent in the three sides of the labyrinth.

Although each part of the wheel has its own meaning, the symbol itself represents the transfer of energy and knowledge through divine forces. The Strophalos of Hekate are connected to the Chaldean Oracles, associated with the Neoplatonic metaphysical belief. This belief states that an all-knowing and all-powerful Father with unlimited divine powers and intellect created the universe. He is the main source of all wisdom in the cosmos.

This Father has his own ambassadors who are responsible for transmitting wisdom and knowledge to mankind. Hekate is one of his emissaries who delivers this information to Earth so everyone can benefit from it. Each part of the symbol has a different meaning related to this transmission of knowledge.

### The Labyrinth

The labyrinth symbolizes the different stages of human life that every person must go through. During this journey, one should absorb the knowledge of the universe before their life ends and their spirit returns to its Maker. The labyrinth also represents the self-discovery that one undergoes in life. It can also be described as a loop that signifies the circle of life and its three stages.p

### Life

The first cycle is life, and it represents birth. The spirit spends this stage bound to the physical body.

### Death

The second cycle is death. It happens after the physical body withers and is separated from the spirit. The spirit then ascends to a different plane of existence, the realm of the dead, where it spends the rest of eternity.

### Rebirth

The last stage is rebirth. After the spirit ascends, it can reach a higher state of being and experience enlightenment. The spirit should then go through a rebirth where it either reincarnates and lives again in the physical form or returns to its Divine Father.

### The Star

The star is another part of the Hekate. It is placed in the center and represents the Divine Father, who is omniscient and the source of all knowledge. The six sides of the star symbolize the spark that ignites in one's soul and connects you to the world around you and the Divine Father.

There are other forms of the wheel with the letters X or Y at its center instead of the star. The letter Y represents the intersection of the three crossroads where Hekate stands guard in her Triple Goddess form.

### The Inner Circle

The inner circle is the first circle in the Hekate wheel. It symbolizes the goddess herself, who is the guardian and protector of divine knowledge and the one who distributes it among mankind by being a reflection of the divinity of the Creator.

## The Outer Circle

The second circle and the last part of the wheel form the outer circle, symbolizing the limitations of the energy Hekate uses when transferring Divine knowledge to humans. An enclosed area between the two circles represents the space between the intellectual and physical worlds. Hekate uses this space to spread the Divine information.

The wheel also symbolizes the concepts of renewal and rebirth since it is related to the shape of the labyrinthine serpent, which rotates in a spiral form. In Greek mythology, the serpent has different meanings and is often depicted with other deities. For instance, snakes are engraved on the staves of Asclepius, the god of medicine, and Hermes, the god of fertility and language, representing medicine and healing.

Hekate is also often depicted with snakes which symbolize fertility and rebirth. In one of the ancient Greek creation myths, the world was created by a giant snake that incubated an egg. Snakes shed their skin every few years and come out with new and rejuvenated bodies. For this reason, serpents represent rebirth and the idea that every creature can be reborn differently.

The spiral part of the symbol is responsible for transmitting Divine knowledge to mankind through rituals like turning the wheels of the Strophalos to release a sound. If one performs this ritual after the death of someone, Hekate will respond to this sound and come down to help the spirit of the deceased ascend to the Divine Father.

The spiral and other parts of the Strophalos are associated with rituals related to the Divine. They usually attract the Divine Father and Hekate and can also be used to perform various spells. The sound it releases resembles the movements and sounds of the iynges, enchanting mediums and tools connected with the Divine intellect.

# Using the Hekate Wheel

The Hekate wheel is one of the major symbols of the goddess since it is used to call on her and invoke her powers. It is a very popular symbol among Wiccans and Neopagans. Hekate represents feminine energy because of its association with the three stages of womanhood and the moon's energy. For this reason, women can invoke the goddess during any stage of their lives.

Besides being a symbol of divine knowledge, the wheel also represents the journey of the human spirit. Each person must go through each part of the symbol by experiencing the ups, downs, and complexities of life under the guidance and protection of Hekate until one reaches the final stage, which is the center of the wheel, and finally achieve enlightenment.

Nowadays, people use the Hekate wheel for religious purposes. Practitioners of various religions, like Hellenic Reconstructionism, a Neopagan tradition inspired by ancient Greek beliefs, also incorporate the wheel into their practices. Many women also wear the wheel as jewelry, like necklaces or bracelets, or even have them tattooed on their bodies because they believe it can bring wealth, success, and good luck into their lives by creating a connection between them and Hekate.

# Facts about the Hekate Wheel

- If you see someone wearing the wheel, they are probably practitioners of the Dianic Traditions of Wicca.
- Many feminists also wear or use the wheel because it is associated with the Triple Goddess and the three stages of femininity.
- The three parts in the labyrinth always look as if they are rotating. This represents drawing forward one's psyche to connect with Divine wisdom.
- The wheel is sometimes called "*iynx*," and one can use it as a divinatory tool, a devotional wheel, or to bring love into their life.
- Sometimes, devotees place the wheel over their heads and let it whirl to create a sound that drives predators away and increases their awareness.
- Essentially, the wheel serves as a reminder that Hekate is by your side, guiding you through your journey in the physical world.

### The Hekate Wheel and the Iynx

Although iynx is another name for the Hekate wheel, some argue that the two are different symbols associated with the goddess. "Iynx" is derived from "*iunx*," Greek for the *wryneck bird*, a type of woodpecker bird that feeds on ants. Originally, people used the iynx wheel to perform spells. The wheel's rotation makes a sound similar to an iunx's call.

The iynx wheel is associated with Aphrodite and her son Eros, more commonly known as Cupid and the god of physical desire and passion. Both used the wheel to attract lovers and bring them together. The iynx is also associated with Hekate, as is clear in one of the poems by the Greek poet Theocritus. He told the story of a woman who went to a sorcerer and asked him to return her unfaithful lover. The practitioner used the iynx wheel to cast the spell and invoked Hekate.

Understandably, you can be confused when Hekate is called on in love spells since she has dominion over aspects unrelated to romance. However, many stories in Greek mythology and literature talk about how the goddess was called on to assist with matters of the heart.

The iynx wheel is also associated with funerals and death, another reason it's considered a symbol for Hekate.

### Dogs

Hekate is often portrayed with dogs. In Greek mythology, dogs would bark at night to announce the goddess's arrival on Earth. They also howl when she or any of her followers use magic. She can even take the form of a dog.

Hekate's dogs were first depicted as quiet and friendly creatures. However, just like the goddess underwent some changes through the years, so did her pets. They came to represent angry spirits or demons. Similar to the mysterious shift in Hekate, no one knows exactly why the depictions of her dogs also changed.

One can say that the dogs resemble Hekate as they also have dark and light sides. They can be dangerous and scary creatures or provide assistance and protection.

One of her dogs was originally the Trojan queen Hecuba. After Troy fell, Hecuba was captured, thrown off a cliff, and died instantly. Hekate felt sorry for the dead queen and brought her back to life as a dog who became a loyal companion to the goddess for eternity.

Hekate is also associated with other animals like:

- Boars
- Snakes
- Bats
- Lambs
- Sheep
- Horses

## Polecat

Hekate is associated with polecats, and she is usually depicted with them. The reason behind this association goes back to an old legend that tells the story of Heracles' (the divine hero) birth.

One of Zeus's mortal lovers, Alcmene, was pregnant with his son Heracles. When his wife Hera found out, she was very jealous and wanted to get rid of the child before he was born. She sent the Moirae Sisters (the Fates) and Eileithyia, the goddess of childbirth, to close off Alcmene's womb. When her handmaid, Galinthias, discovered what the goddesses did, she lied to them by saying that Alcmene had already given birth. Moirae and Eileithyia fell for the trick and let go of their hold on Alcmene's womb, and she gave birth. They punished her by turning her into a polecat when they found out that Galinthias lied to them.

Galinthias led a terrible life as a polecat. She had to hide in dirty holes and struggled to survive. When Hekate learned about the poor maid's fate, she sympathized with her. She tried to reverse the curse but failed, making the polecat one of her sacred attendants.

## Keys

Hekate is often depicted holding keys, and because of that, she is described as the keeper of keys. These are believed to be the keys to the universe that can unlock its mysteries, magic, and healing powers. Other scholars argue that these are the keys to the crossroads. Since she is the goddess of the crossroads and stands guard over them, she holds these keys to provide protection and prevent danger from entering. They are also believed to be the keys to the underworld, where she has dominion. Hekate uses this key to unlock the mysteries of the afterlife and the secrets of the occult.

During certain rituals, Hekate priestesses often carry keys to represent the goddess's role as the keeper of keys.

Everyone uses keys to unlock their car, home, office, etc., and some even use keys in their decor or wear them as jewelry. If you consider these keys to be symbols of Hekate, you can constantly feel that she is with you and providing protection through one of her symbols.

## Crossroads

Hekate is the goddess of the crossroads, so naturally, they are one of her symbols. Boundaries can cause limitations in your daily life and set obstacles you must overcome to grow. Hekate's role as the goddess of the crossroads is to mediate these boundaries.

Crossroads can also represent the many daily choices, like which road to take, which job to apply to, or which decisions to make. Crossroads are also associated with the future, present, and past. In her triple form, Hekate can see each of the three crossroads, representing the past, present, and future. Therefore, she is in a perfect position to provide guidance and help one make better choices.

## Triple Form

Hekate is a Triple goddess. Many of her statues and illustrations show her in her triple form. Like Hermes, the messenger of the gods, people placed her statues near borders and crossroads in ancient Greece to ward off misfortune, harm, and evil.

## Daggers

In modern times and among Neo-pagans, Hekate is depicted with three torches, six arms, and sacred symbols: a dagger, rope, and a key. The dagger symbolizes the goddess's dominion over magic and witchcraft. It is also used to ward off evil spirits and perform ritualistic spells. For the followers of Hekate, the dagger can bring you to trust your inner voice and judgment, provide empowerment, and protect you from illusions.

## Ropes

Hekate usually carries a rope, representing the umbilical cord, a symbol of renewal and rebirth. The rope is also called a scourge or a cord.

## Triple Moon

As the triple moon goddess, Hekate is associated with the moon's dark side. If you remember from science class, the moon is a dark body, and its light reflects the sunlight. Hekate represents the moon's darkness in its true form, especially during the new moon phase.

## Torches

Hekate is usually depicted holding two torches, one in each hand, to represent her role as a protector and provide guidance. She would light up the way for those struggling with obstacles and difficulties on their daily journey so they could see clearly and reach their destination.

Her torches were featured in a few legends. For instance, during the war between the Giants and the Olympian gods, she used her torch to kill the giant Clytius and help the gods win the war.

The torches are some of Hekate's most significant symbols, making her powerful and adding to her mysteries and contradictions. For a goddess associated with the dark aspects of life, like the underworld and the dark side of the moon, she is also a force of light.

One can always call on Hekate to light the darkness inside them or when they are facing obstacles and looking for someone to show them the way and illuminate their dark roads.

### Serpents

In various illustrations, Hekate is depicted with a serpent in her hand. In ancient Greece, serpents were associated with necromancy and magic. People used them in spells to detect the presence of a spirit.

### Crescent

The crescent has been a symbol of Hekate ever since Roman times. Back then, people saw her as mainly a moon goddess, so the crescent became her symbol to signify her connection with the moon.

### Owls

In some illustrations, Hekate is depicted surrounded by owls which symbolize wisdom. Although she isn't the goddess of wisdom, she is still associated with it. For starters, as the goddess of the crossroads, she can see into the past, present, and future, possessing knowledge of each stage of one's life. She also has access to the Divine wisdom she spread among the people, so having owls as her symbol represents these different aspects of the goddess.

### Willows

There are many symbols associated with willow trees. They signify survival, adaptability, hope, growth, change, and new beginnings. Since Hekate is the goddess of the crossroads, she represents new beginnings and change, which makes the willow tree her ideal symbol.

The goddess is associated with other plants as well.

- Pumpkins
- Currants
- Raisins
- Saffron
- Blackthorn
- Dark yew
- Groves of trees

## Scents

Since Hekate is the goddess of the moon and is associated with night, she is often called the "Queen of the night." This makes the queen of the night flower an appropriate symbol of the goddess. The flowers are just as mysterious as Hekate because they bloom simultaneously, making them quite intriguing. In some cultures, if you pray to a deity or make a wish while the queen of the night is blooming, your wish or prayer will come true.

Other scents that are associated with Hekate:

- Lemon verbena
- Lime
- Honey
- Mugwort
- Myrrh
- Cinnamon

## Colors

Hekate is associated with the color black. This makes sense for a goddess who represents the night, darkness, the underworld, and death. Black is also a mysterious color, so it perfectly fits the intriguing goddess.

Hekate is also associated with red-orange, yellow-orange, and orange.

## Metals and Gems

Luminous and dark stones symbolize Hekate as they represent the dark aspects of the goddess's personality.

The gems and metals Hekate is associated with include:

- Smoky quartz
- Hematite
- Black onyx
- Black Tourmaline
- Moonstone
- Gold
- Silver
- Sapphire

## Practical Exercise

Now that you have become familiar with Hekate's symbols, *try drawing your own*. You can draw the wheel in any of its forms or create something from your imagination using any of her symbols. Don't use Google to find ideas; let your intuition guide you instead and draw what feels right. Sit in a quiet room without distractions, get a blank piece of paper, hold a pen or pencil, and start drawing.

The symbols of Hekate reflect the many contradictions and mysteries around the goddess. She is associated with dark colors and metals and the dark side of the moon, yet she is depicted with a torch in her hand to provide light and guidance. Her symbols also showcase her significant role in one's life. She isn't only the goddess of witchcraft and the underworld. Still, she has the power to transfer Divine knowledge among mankind and can see into the future.

There are many sides to Hekate's personality and different aspects to worshiping her. One can use her symbols to cast spells, seek guidance, ask for protection, pray for wisdom, and various other things. Hecake is more than just a dark goddess associated with witchcraft; she can also be a force of light, helping you overcome obstacles and illuminating the darkest roads.

# Chapter 4: Connecting with Hekate

You've now learned about Hekate and her associations; you're probably eager to make contact with her. This chapter will help you explore different methods of connecting – from journeying to her and meeting her at the crossroads to meditating with her and expressing your gratitude for her presence to mindfulness techniques that will bring the two of you together. You'll explore all the meaningful ways to bond with Hekate, preparing you for other practical techniques for working with the goddess (to be described in the subsequent chapters).

## Important Disclaimers

Before you delve into the practical side of working with Hekate, you must consider a few things. The first one is your **mental health**. Witchcraft and rituals require intense focus and mental strength. Not only that, but working with Hekate also means that you'll experience changes in your life, which can make you vulnerable to negative influences. Remember, she is an incredibly powerful goddess and a witch who can land you plenty of spiritual and magical power - but you must be ready to accept it. You must be able to ward off the negative energies to overcome your difficulties.

All this is only possible if you have sound mental health. If you're already having issues with your mental health, you likely won't be able to focus on your intentions. In the best-case scenario, you won't be able to connect with Hekate. You'll only waste your mental energy when you could've used it for mental and spiritual healing. In the worst-case scenario, you'll have a bad experience (like disturbing visions and dreams), which will further contribute to the decline of your mental health.

So, if you've experienced mental health issues in the past, focus on healing before attempting to make contact with Hekate. Symptoms to watch out for include lack of sleep and other sleep disturbances, problems with memory, fatigue, depression, and anxiety. Furthermore, if you notice any of these symptoms after you've begun to work with Hekate, stop, and seek help from a medical professional to treat your symptoms. Don't continue until you've improved your mental well-being.

The next factor to consider is **fire safety.** Working with Hekacte often requires using candles, small torches, or other sources of fire. Never leave the flames unattended. If you're finished with them for a while and plan to leave the space, extinguish the fire. You can relight it when you return and dedicate time to supervise it again. Another reason you should leave flames burning for long periods is that the rituals you need them for require focus. You can focus on an intention for only so long - once your concentration declines, your work becomes ineffective. Relighting the flames is more effective when you return with a fresh mind and are ready to focus on your intention again. Avoid using open sources of fire near small children, pets, or in unventilated spaces. The focus the magical work requires can divert your attention from supervising the pets or children. This can prevent you from being able to stop them if they get too close to the flames. Working with flames in a ventilated space forms a better connection with Hekate. Not to mention it's much safer for you, your home, and those around you. Fire uses oxygen, which you'll also need. Working in a ventilated space will provide you with plenty of oxygen, and with all that oxygen cursing through your body and mind, you'll be able to focus better.

Lastly, you should keep in mind that working with Hekate requires **the use of herbs.** While the herbs the goddess uses have health benefits, they can also have adverse effects. Always consult a medical health professional before ingesting any herbs or using them topically. The same applies to essential oils, too - these contain herbal compounds in a concentrated form, so they can have an even greater impact on your health. When talking to your doctor, pharmacist, or an experienced herbalist about herbs or herbal blends you plan to use, mention if you have any preexisting conditions. Some illnesses represent a contraindication for herbs used when working with Hekate. If you experience any side effects - such as skin irritations, nausea, or changes in breathing, blood pressure, or heart arrhythmia - after ingesting or topically applying the herbs, seek immediate medical attention. Stop using the herbs in any form until your health issues are resolved.

*Now that the disclaimers are out of the way, you can delve into the different techniques for connecting with Hekate.* As this will be your first time contacting and working with the goddess, the following approaches have a meditational format. Medication and mindfulness techniques are proven to improve focus. They'll teach you how to concentrate on your intention in future work. Below are a few approaches to bonding with Hekate and tips on making them work for you. Remember, working with the goddess of transformation is highly personal. While following the techniques below can be a sound way to start, they'll only have full effects if you make them your own.

## Journeying to Meet Hekate

This meditation will help you meet and communicate with Hekate at her sacred crossroads. You'll stay in one place for 8-10 minutes, so make sure to find a comfortable position and support for your back if needed. Here is how to start the journey to meet Hekate:

1. Assume a comfortable position - preferably sitting cross-legged. Alternatively, you can lie down on a mat. Rest your hand on your legs and ensure your back is relaxed.

2. Take three deep breaths. When doing this, use your abdominal muscles. That way, your breathing becomes even deeper. Every time you inhale, exhale slowly with a long, audible sigh.

3. After the third exhale, examine your body to see if you're relaxed and comfortable or need to adjust your position.

4. Close your eyes and picture yourself walking along a dark, graveled path on a quiet night. Visualize a waning moon rising over the tree lines. You can only hear the sound of the night - crickets in nearby bushes and the call of an owl reaching you from a faraway tree.

5. Keep walking confidently forward in your vision, and try to enjoy the solitude and companionship of the sound the crunching gravel makes beneath your feet. It's cold, and you can see the little puffs

your breath makes in the chill of the late evening air.

6. As you walk, picture a flickering light up ahead of you. As you get closer, you'll see the light coming from a torch marking the crossroads. The closer you get, the more detailed the image becomes. You can see offerings left by other devotees at the signpost.

7. Next, visualize a small offering you're carrying in your hands. This could be a small bundle of homemade bread, an apple, or anything else that comes to mind.

8. As you reach the crossroads, the wind picks up, carrying a swirl of roads across the crossroads. Stop for a moment to take in the captivating scene. Approach the torchlight area as quietly as possible.

9. Take a deep breath and leave your offering while saying a quiet prayer to Hekate. As you do, start focusing on your surroundings. While you're perfectly comfortable being alone at night, you suddenly pick up a source of energy in the air.

10. As you try to figure out where the energy comes from, you suddenly hear howling dogs. The wind becomes even stronger, making you gasp as it swirls around you, and you battle to see what's happening. You feel the earth tremble beneath your feet and hear a deep rumbling noise. If you feel unstable, visualize yourself grabbing the signpost to keep yourself upright.

11. Now, picture the noise and the winds fading away and the night becoming silent and peaceful again. Your offering is now on the ground. However, as you turn slowly, you realize you're not alone.

12. Next, visualize a large black dog running to you and affectionately greeting you. Feel free to pet the dog and play with it, giving in to the laughter the free spirit of animals often brings out from people. As you're scratching the dog's ears, it suddenly signals that someone is approaching - a woman dressed in an elaborate black hooded cape.

13. As you see the woman approaching silently on her sandal-clad feet, an owl flies in and lands gracefully on the top of the signpost. It blinks its wide eyes at you and ruffles its feathers. Nervous, you prepare to greet the woman by bowing your head. After greeting her, you look up to discover that she is a regal-looking middle-aged woman wearing a silver crown. However, as you continue looking

at her, her face starts to change - first to a young woman, then to a much older one with white hair.

14. Focus on the woman's eyes - they're black and radiate with timeless wisdom. Visualize her greeting you and thanking you for visiting her in her sacred place. While she might look intimidating, try not to be afraid of her. This will prompt her to reassure you that she will not bring you death or misfortune. Instead, she will assist you through any changes upon you and escort you to the next stage of your life.

15. Picture her giving you tree keys as gifts. These represent knowledge, intuition, and magic. Hekate instructs you to hold these gifts close to your heart and not hesitate to call on her when you need her. Feel the warmth coursing through your body when you raise the keys to your heart and whisper your thanks.

16. Lastly, visualize Hekate turning away and slowly walking away from you, accompanied by her dog and owl. A mist seems to swallow them up as you let their image disappear from your view. The last image in your vision should be that of the signpost - should you ever wish to return there, it will be waiting for you.

17. Take a deep breath, grounding yourself again, and let the journey take you back home. As you find yourself back in your room, bring your attention back to your breath. Take three slow, audible breaths to bring yourself all the way back. Have a stretch, and when you feel ready, open your eyes and slowly return to your everyday activities.

# Meditating on a Symbol

Meditation allows you to connect with Hekate.
*https://unsplash.com/photos/V-TIPBoC_2M*

One of the easiest ways to connect with Hekate is through one of her symbols. Draw it on a piece of paper and meditate with it to bring the goddess's energy closer to you. Here is how to do it:

1. Start by assuming a comfortable position in a quiet room at night. Make sure that you won't be disturbed for at least 10-15 minutes before you start your meditation.

2. Take the symbol of your hands and great the goddess:

   *"Goddess Hekate, Queen of all Witches*

   *Host of the underworld and things unseen*

   *Custodian of crossroads and liminal places*

   *Queen of dead and transforming spaces*

   *The Soul of night animals and moonlight*

   *I greet you this night."*

3. Visualize the symbol in front of your eyes (or keep looking at it on the paper - whichever helps you more).

4. Take a few breaths and focus on feeling a potent energy source emanating from the symbol.

---

5. Feel the goddess's energy reaching you, enveloping your body, carrying Hekate's gifts. Feel it empowering you, preparing you for your subsequent challenges, and lifting you up spiritually.

6. Continue focusing on the energy of the symbol until you feel prepared to complete your meditation.

7. When ready, let the image of the symbol with the energy fade away (and let the paper fall from your hands if you were holding it).

8. Exhale deeply, and let your mind return to your mundane thoughts.

# Meditating in the Dark

This night-time meditation focuses on embracing the dark home of Hekate and inviting her into your world. As with any other meditation or mindfulness technique, you start by getting comfortable in a place where you won't be disturbed. For practical purposes, choosing a place near your altar where you can place a candle and light it for Hekate is recommended. Here is how to perform this mediation:

1. After lighting a candle, turning off all the lights, and assuming a comfortable position, take a deep breath.

2. As you exhale, let go of any tension you feel in your body and allow your mind to sink into a state of relaxedness and ease.

3. Focusing on the candle flame, let your everyday thoughts drift far away. Visualize them floating away until you can't see them with your mind's eye.

4. Take another slow deep breath and focus on feeling safe in the here and now as you prepare to travel into the deep night. There, you'll meet Hekate and reveal the deepest parts of yourself.

5. Picture yourself wrapped in a long cloak - feeling safe under the goddess's protection. As you look away from your black velvet cloak, you suddenly see yourself in a lush, green, earthy meadow at night. You start exploring the meadow as the sounds of the night accompany you.

6. Visualize an entrance in a tree nearby the meadow. As you approach the entrance, you'll see five stairs leading to a gate guarded by three black dogs. As you descend the steps, you start feeling the divine energy reaching out to you, making you more confident in your purpose.

7. As you reach the entrance, tap into your mind, and look for painful memories you wish to leave behind. Acknowledging each one, offer these memories to the guardian dogs.

8. You'll feel lighter as you see the dogs burying your memories deep into the ground. The animals allow you to pass and meet Hekate.

9. Picture the goddess in front of you, dressed in the same black robe you are - the symbol of her energy residing within you. She offers her protection, and you accept it. Take in her picture and know that just as she survived many challenges, so will you until your soul's journey in this life is over.

10. Before you leave her side, offer the goddess a small token of gratitude as an offering. This could be a thought of worthlessness, prejudice, or any negative emotion you want to leave behind. Imagine Hekate placing these thoughts and feelings into a blue cauldron, where they disappear into the smoke of the magic she is brewing.

11. To fill the space left behind by the negative thoughts and emotions, Hekate offers you her blessings. Accept them and feel your body and mind relaxed and safe as they reach you.

12. As her energy seeps into your darkest secret, take three deep breaths and let the emotions that come with the secret break free. Embrace any emotions you feel - sadness, rage, anxiety, etc. - in the here and now.

13. Now imagine these feelings as rooms in your consciousness. As the magic from the goddess continues emanating towards your body and mind, they reach the dark rooms, swallowing the negative emotions and leaving nothing behind.

14. Continue reminiscing on the effects of the healing energy until you're ready to return. Then, take three slow, easy breaths and thank Hekate for her gifts and healing. Turn away from the goddess, and walk back up the stairs through the meadow, slowly bringing awareness back to the present.

15. Once you're ready, open your eyes and feel revitalized and filled with positive energy.

# Reading the Orphic Hymn to Hekate

1. Reading the Orphic Hymn to Hekate (you'll find this in the bonus chapter) is another splendid way to express your intention of meeting them and working with them. Here is how to offer this hymn in a few simple steps:

2. Light a purple candle on your altar. Place offerings and symbols of the goddess around the candle. Keep the text of the hymn within your reach.

3. Get comfortable in front of the altar. Gaze into the candle and focus on relaxing your mind and body.

4. Take a few deep breaths, then start reading the hymn. Do it slowly, and when you reach the end, pause, and look into the candle flame again. Repeat this two more times.

5. By the time you're finished with the last repetition, night has fallen, and you're ready to go to bed. As you do, prepare for a restful sleep with the goddess's blessings.

# Hekate Mediation at a Threshold

Meditating at a threshold is the easiest way to reach Hekate's sacred crossroads as a beginner. Make sure the threshold you're using is undisturbed so you can focus on the exercise without interruption. Here is how to meditate with Hekate at a threshold:

1. Start at dusk. This is a time of transition when the goddess's power is at its strongest. Turn off all the lights and electronic devices nearby, and sit near the threshold. Lean your back against something supporting it, and place a cushion behind it. You can also cover yourself with a cozy blanket, as it might get chilly.

2. Take a deep breath and close your eyes. When you're ready, picture yourself walking uphill toward a beautiful patch of nature. Despite the approaching darkness, you can see that the grass is vivid green, just like the crown of the trees.

3. You feel a light breeze and the scent of the woods as you easily stroll toward the trees. As you pass them, up ahead, you'll see light coming from beyond the trees. Imagine yourself walking towards the light and suddenly reaching the top of the hill, which is also a cliff. Down below, you can see the dark ocean.

4. Instead of a steep pathway leading down the cliff, imagine a gently curving path leading to the ocean. Take this path, and feel yourself relaxing with each step.

5. When you reach the bottom of the hill, you feel sand under your feet. It's soft and gentle, and as you stroll along the beach, you hear the sound of the waves meeting the sand.

6. Further down the beach, you see a cave. Stroll towards it, and don't fear entering it. Take a few deep breaths if you need to calm yourself. Feel the soothing energy emanating from the cave as the goddess invites you into her home.

7. Picture yourself entering a brightly lit cave. As your eyes adjust to the lights, you'll see that the cave is much deeper than it seemed from the outside. From the cave's depths emerges a female figure and reaches what's revealed to be the crossroads.

8. See yourself smiling at Hekate as she smiles back at you and embraces you with her nurturing energy. As you start your journey together, you can ask the goddess what she wants you to know today. If you aren't prepared to ask her anything, you can just stand here, letting her presence relax and empower you.

9. Let the image of Hekate disappear, but you can remain at the crossroads as long as you want to. You can even let yourself drift off to sleep if you wish.

10. When you're ready, leave the cave. As you step outside, let the sounds of the ocean bring you back to reality. Stretch yourself and open your eyes when you feel ready.

# Meeting the Goddess

This is another method for meeting the goddess. It's similar to journeying but a much more straightforward process. However, it requires plenty of concentration. Here is how to do it:

1. Prepare for going to bed. Besides preparing yourself, make sure that your bedroom is as soothing a place as possible, suitable for a relaxing practice and sleep afterward. Avoid using electronics for at least an hour before going to bed. This way, your mind can slowly unwind and focus on the exercise.

2. When you're ready, turn off the lights and lie down. Feel comfortable and close your eyes.

3. Take a few deep breaths until you feel your mind and body relaxing.
4. Visualize yourself walking down a dark tunnel slowly while calling on the goddess. See her appear before you at the other end of the tunnel.
5. Say a few words of greeting and gratitude for their presence.
6. Slowly let the vision fade away, take a deep breath, and let yourself fall asleep naturally.

# Chapter 5: Hekatean Herblore

In Greek mythology, the goddess Hekate was revered as the queen of witches and the guardian of the crossroads. Her power was said to extend beyond the physical realm and into the spiritual, where she was known to guide and protect those who asked for her help. However, the most significant aspect of Hekate's domain was her connection to herbs and their mystical properties. According to legends, Hekate was an expert in herbal knowledge and created various herbal concoctions that could bring about extraordinary changes in the natural world. These herbal infusions were said to be filled with Hekate's sacred energy, which could be used to heal or harm, depending on the practitioner's intentions. The herbs associated with Hekate hold the key to unlocking and manifesting the witch goddess's potent magic. For instance, Mugwort, a favorite herb of the goddess, was often burned as incense during rituals and rites to call upon her powers.

People who sought Hekate's guidance and help in matters of the heart and spirit often turned to herbs associated with her to communicate with the goddess. It was believed that certain plants, such as mandrake or datura, could open a channel of communication between the physical and spiritual realms, allowing one to connect with the goddess directly. In this chapter, you will explore the many herbs associated with Hekate and the intricate web of myth and magic surrounding them. From their historical uses to their use in modern Wiccan rituals, you will delve into the world of herblore and discover the secrets of Hekate's mystical garden.

# Herbs Associated with Hekate

The herbs associated with Hekate are as diverse as they are potent. Each one is said to hold a unique connection to the goddess and her power, making them a crucial part of any practitioner's toolkit. These include:

## 1. Yew

Yew is a tree with a long history of being associated with magic and mysticism. Due to its potent properties and symbolic significance, many cultures have considered it sacred. In Wiccan and Hekatean cultures, yew is a particularly powerful plant that has a special connection to the goddess, Hekate. The yew tree symbolizes death and the underworld. In Greek mythology, it was believed that the yew was sacred to Hekate because it grew near the entrance to the underworld. The tree was seen as a portal between the physical and spiritual realms and was considered a conduit for communicating with the goddess. Historically, yew has been used in various cultures as a means of divination and protection. Druids in ancient Britain considered the yew to be a sacred tree and used its branches in their magical practices. The ancient Celts also believed it had the power to protect against evil spirits and curses.

The yew tree has been associated with mysticism.
https://pixabay.com/es/photos/tejo-tejo-ingl%c3%a9s-frutos-rojos-6678612/

In modern times, yew is still used in various forms of spellwork and ritual. One popular way to use yew is to create an incense blend that can be burned during ceremonies to honor Hekate or to call upon her power. To make a yew incense blend, combine dried yew leaves with other herbs and resins associated with the goddess, such as mugwort, frankincense, and myrrh. Another way to incorporate yew into your magical practice is to create a protection pouch. To do this, carve a small piece of yew wood into a shape representing Hekate or one of her symbols, such as a key or a torch. Place the carved wood in a small pouch along with other protective herbs and crystals, such as black tourmaline or sage. This pouch can be carried with you or placed in a specific area of your home to create a protective barrier.

## 2. Cypress

The cypress tree is one of the most enigmatic and intriguing trees in the natural world. It stands tall and imposing, starkly contrasting with the gentle, weeping willows that sway in the breeze. For centuries, the cypress has been linked to the goddess Hekate, and its symbolism and mythology make it a powerful addition to any magical practice. This tree is often associated with the concept of transformation, particularly regarding Hekate's herblore. In Greek mythology, it was believed that Hekate was the goddess of transitions - the guide and protector of souls as they moved from one world to the next. With its tall, dark silhouette, the cypress was seen as a symbol of this journey, with the tree's roots reaching down into the underworld.

The Cypress tree is associated with transformation.
https://pixabay.com/es/photos/cipreses-toscana-paisaje-avenida-3701931/

The cypress is a tree that has long been linked to the concept of purification. In ancient times, people would burn the tree's wood and needles to cleanse their homes and protect themselves from negative energy. Today, cypress essential oil is still used in many spiritual and magical practices to purify and cleanse the environment. This oil can be added to bathwater, diffused in a room, or used in a homemade cleansing spray. The cypress is also said to have protective properties, making it a popular ingredient in many spells and rituals. Its energy is considered especially powerful regarding matters of the heart and relationships. Some practitioners use its oil to create a protective charm for a loved one or to promote self-love and healing.

If you want to incorporate cypress into your magical practice, there are many ways to do so. You can create an altar dedicated to Hekate and adorn it with cypress branches, cones, and candles. You can also use its wood to create a wand or staff that you can use to channel the goddess's transformative energy. For a more subtle touch, simply carry a piece of cypress wood in your pocket to keep the goddess's energy close to you throughout the day.

### 3. Witch Hazel

Witch hazel, also known as winter bloom, is a flowering shrub that is associated with the goddess Hekate in her role as a healer and protector. Witch hazel has long been used in traditional medicine for its anti-inflammatory, astringent, and soothing properties, making it a powerful addition to any magical practice. Hekate's association with witch hazel is linked to its healing properties and ability to cleanse and purify. Ancient magic practitioners often called upon the goddess to help heal the sick and injured, and witch hazel was used in many of these healing rituals. Its astringent properties were used to treat skin conditions, while its anti-inflammatory properties were used to reduce swelling and pain.

**Witch hazel cleanses and purifies.**
*Si Griffiths, CC BY-SA 3.0 DEED < https://creativecommons.org/licenses/by-sa/3.0/deed.en>, via Wikimedia Commons https://commons.wikimedia.org/wiki/File:Witch-hazel_(Hamamelis)_In_Flower._RHS_Wisley_Garden_Surrey_UK.jpg*

In Hekate's herblore, witch hazel is also associated with protection and banishing negative energy. Its cleansing properties are said to purify spaces and remove any unwanted energy or spirits. The shrub's branches and leaves can create a protective barrier or ward off evil spirits around the home. If you wish to incorporate witch hazel into your magical practice, there are many ways to do so. You can create a witch hazel infusion for healing spells or to cleanse and purify your home.

You can also use the shrub's leaves and branches in a protection spell or charm, carrying it with you to ward off negative energy and protect you from harm. You can create a witch hazel-based spray for banishing spells by mixing witch hazel extract with essential oils known for their banishing properties, such as sage, cedarwood, or rosemary. Simply spray the mixture around your home or on your person to banish negative energy and spirits.

### 4. Black Poplar

The black poplar, also known as Populus nigra, is a species of tree strongly associated with Hekate, the Greek goddess of witchcraft, magic, and the night. The tree's connection to the goddess can be traced back to ancient times when it was believed that the rustling of the leaves was the voice of the goddess herself. Black poplar is associated with transformation, renewal, and the mysteries of death and rebirth. The tree's tall and slender stature, with its roots planted firmly in the underworld, symbolizes the goddess's connection to the spiritual world and the mysteries of the afterlife. The black poplar was also believed to be a source of divination, as its leaves and branches were used to make oracular pronouncements.

**Black poplar is used for transformation and renewal.**
*David Hawgood / Black Poplar, near Milton Common, CC BY-SA 2.0 DEED <*
*https://creativecommons.org/licenses/by-sa/2.0/deed.en> via Wikimedia Commons*
*https://commons.wikimedia.org/wiki/File:Black_Poplar,_near_Milton_Common_-*
*_geograph.org.uk_-_245091.jpg*

Historically, the black poplar was used in a variety of magical rituals and spells, particularly those related to transformation and renewal. Its bark and leaves were used to make teas, tinctures, and poultices to aid in healing and help with life transitions, such as birth, death, and spiritual awakening. The tree's wood was also used to create wands, believed to help the practitioner connect with the energies of transformation and change. Today, black poplar is still used in magical practices to aid in transformation and renewal. Its leaves can be dried and burned as incense to help with meditation and connect with the goddess's transformative energy. The bark and leaves can also be used to create tea, which can be consumed to aid in spiritual healing and help with transitions in life.

### 5. Garlic

With its potent aroma and powerful properties, garlic has long been associated with Hekate. In Hekate's herblore, garlic is known as a protective herb that can banish negativity and evil spirits. In ancient times, garlic was believed to be a potent weapon against dark forces and malevolent spirits. Its strong scent was thought to be harmful to evil beings and that it could drive them away. For this reason, it was often placed at the entrance to homes or hung in windows to ward off negative energies.

Garlic is used to keep dark forces and spirits away.
https://unsplash.com/photos/vIiye0QDryo

In Hekate's magic, garlic is used to protect the practitioner from harm and to banish negative energy. Its pungent scent is said to clear the air of negativity and create a protective barrier around the practitioner. It can be used in a variety of magical workings, from creating protective charms to adding it to food for its magical properties. Today, garlic is still a powerful tool in modern magical practices. It can be used to create protective sachets or amulets, added to cleansing baths, or burned as incense to create a protective atmosphere. It can also be used in culinary magic, where its flavor and magical properties can be incorporated into recipes to promote healing and protection.

### 6. Lavender

Lavender, with its soft purple hues and delicate fragrance, is a beloved herb in the world of magic and folklore. It is said to have been associated with Hekate, the Greek goddess of witchcraft, for its calming properties and ability to soothe the mind and spirit. In Hekate's herblore, lavender is often used in spells and rituals to promote peace, harmony, and balance. Its gentle energy is said to align the chakras and calm the mind, making it a powerful tool for meditation and divination. Lavender's association with Hekate is also tied to its connection to the moon. Hekate is often depicted as a lunar goddess, and lavender is believed to be ruled by the moon. The herb's delicate purple flowers are said to represent the moon's gentle glow, while its calming properties mirror the moon's soothing energy.

**Lavender is used to calm and soothe the mind.**
https://unsplash.com/photos/CJWvcrkBhMY

In addition to its magical properties, lavender is a popular herb in aromatherapy and herbal medicine. Its soothing fragrance is believed to have a calming effect on the nervous system, making it a popular remedy for anxiety, stress, and insomnia. To incorporate lavender into your magical practice, you can use it in various ways, from creating herbal sachets to burning lavender-scented candles. You can also add lavender to your bathwater to promote relaxation and create a sense of inner peace.

## 7. Myrrh

Myrrh, with its spicy, resinous scent and ancient history, is a powerful herb in the world of magic and mythology. In ancient times, it was highly valued for its healing properties and used as a currency in some cultures. Myrrh is associated with the underworld and the afterlife in Hekate's herb lore. Its use in funerary rites dates back to ancient times, and it was often burned as an offering to the gods. As the goddess of witchcraft and the keeper of the keys to the underworld, Hekate is often invoked in rituals involving myrrh.

**Myrrh has powerful healing properties.**

The symbolism of myrrh is also tied to its powerful healing properties. It is often used to banish negative energies and to purify the mind, body, and spirit. It promotes healing, boosts the immune system, and calms the nerves. Myrrh is a versatile herb that can be used in various ways in your magical practice; you can burn it as incense to banish negative energies and to create a protective barrier around yourself or your home. You can add it to an herbal bath to promote healing and purification.

## 8. Mugwort

Mugwort is deeply tied to the world of magic and spirituality. It has long been used in many cultures for its powerful properties and is often associated with the goddess Hekate. In Hekate's herblore, mugwort is seen as a herb of protection, especially for women and travelers. It enhances psychic abilities and opens the third eye, making it a popular herb for divination and lucid dreaming. It is also used to aid in astral projection and enhance intuition.

**Mugwort is often used for lunar rituals.**
*AnemoneProjectors, CC BY-SA 2.0 <https://creativecommons.org/licenses/by-sa/2.0>, via Wikimedia Commons*
*https://commons.wikimedia.org/wiki/File:Mugwort_(Artemisia_vulgaris)_(24244929842).jpg*

Symbolically, mugwort is associated with the moon and the element of air. Its silvery leaves and soft, feathery texture evoke the moon's energy and make it a popular herb for lunar rituals. In addition, its light and airy quality makes it useful for spells and rituals that involve movement and transformation. Mugwort is a versatile herb that can be used in various ways in your magical practice. You can burn mugwort as incense to enhance your psychic abilities and aid in divination. You can add it to a dream pillow to encourage lucid dreaming or drink it as a tea to aid astral projection.

## 9. Cardamom

In Hekate's herblore, cardamom is seen as a herb of transformation and protection. It is said to have the power to dispel negative energy and attract positive energy. As a spice highly valued in ancient times, cardamom has a long history of use in various forms of magic, including incense and spells. It was a popular herb in ancient Egyptian and Greek magic and Ayurvedic medicine. It was believed to have healing properties and was used to treat various ailments, including digestive issues and respiratory problems. It was also used as an aphrodisiac and was thought to increase sexual potency.

Cardamom attracts positive energy.
https://unsplash.com/photos/2P0EFD18NYA

In modern magic, cardamom is often used in spells and rituals related to protection, purification, and transformation. It is said to have the power to dispel negative energy and attract positive energy, making it a valuable tool for spiritual practitioners. It can be burned as incense or added to bath water to purify and cleanse the body and mind.

## 10. Mint

In Hekate's herblore, mint is considered a powerful herb of the moon and is often associated with the goddess's association with the underworld. It is believed to help one connect with their intuitive and psychic abilities and is often used in divination and spiritual exploration rituals. Mint has a long history of use in traditional medicine and magic. It was used by the ancient Greeks and Romans to treat various ailments, including digestive issues, headaches, and respiratory problems. It was also used to freshen breath and flavor food.

**Mint is used for rituals and spells for divination and intuition.**
*https://www.pexels.com/photo/green-mint-photo-214165/*

In magic, mint is often used in spells and rituals related to divination, intuition, and spiritual exploration. It is believed to have the power to connect one with the spiritual realm, making it a valuable tool for spiritual practitioners. It can be burned as incense or used in spells to open up one's intuitive abilities and enhance psychic awareness. It is also associated with the element of air, believed to represent the power of communication and intellect. This association with air makes mint a valuable tool for those seeking to improve their communication skills or connect more deeply with the spiritual realm.

## 11. Dandelion

Dandelion is often associated with the Greek goddess Hekate and has been used in her herblore for centuries. The plant is revered for its association with the underworld and its ability to help one connect with their inner power and strength. The bright yellow flowers of the dandelion are believed to represent the power of the sun, while the white, fluffy seeds represent the power of the wind. This combination of solar and lunar energy makes dandelions a powerful tool for transformation and growth, a key aspect of Hekate's association with magic.

**Dandelions represent the power of the sun.**

In ancient times, dandelion was used as a medicinal herb to treat a variety of ailments, including liver problems, digestive issues, and skin conditions. It was also used in divination rituals to help practitioners connect with the spiritual realm and gain insight into their future. In Hekate's herblore, dandelion is often used to enhance intuition, increase psychic abilities, and encourage personal growth and transformation. The herb is believed to help one eliminate old patterns and habits, allowing a more authentic and empowered self to emerge. It is also used in protection spells and rituals, as its association with the underworld and the sun offers powerful protection against negative energies and entities. It can be burned as incense, added to spell bags or sachets, or used in spiritual baths to promote purification and protection.

## 12. Hellebore

Hellebore has long been associated with the Greek goddess Hekate and her magic. It is said to possess powerful energies that can be used to bring about transformation, protection, and connection to the spiritual realm. The hellebore plant has been used in medicinal remedies for thousands of years and was considered a cure for many ailments, including madness, melancholy, and fever. However, its use in magical practices is where its association with Hekate comes in.

Hellebore is used for its protective qualities.
https://pixabay.com/es/photos/helleborus-niger-rosa-de-navidad-7029641/

In Hekate's herblore, hellebore is often used for its protective qualities. It is believed to ward off negative energies, entities, and spirits, making it an important ingredient in spells and rituals of banishing and protection. It is also associated with transformation and rebirth and is used in spells and rituals to help individuals release old patterns and embrace new beginnings. It is a powerful tool for those seeking to connect with the spiritual realm and the wisdom of the goddess.

In addition to its protective and transformative properties, hellebore is associated with divination and prophecy. It enhances one's intuition and psychic abilities, making it an ideal herb for those seeking to develop their spiritual gifts. However, it is important to note that hellebore is poisonous and should not be ingested fresh. It should only be used in its dried form or as an infusion in spiritual baths or washes.

These powerful plants have long been used to connect with the transformative energy of the goddess of the crossroads. From the potent protection of yew to the cleansing and purifying energy of hellebore, each one has its own unique symbolism and magic. When working with these herbs, it is important to honor their power and approach them with respect and intention. Whether you choose to create an incense blend, brew an infusion, or craft a protection pouch, the herbs associated with Hekate offer a powerful tool for connecting with the wisdom and magic of this ancient goddess. As you explore the world of Hekate's herblore, remember that this is just the beginning of a deep and transformative journey. By incorporating these herbs into your magical practice, you can connect with the goddess's energy, embrace your inner power, and unlock the full potential of your spiritual journey.

# Chapter 6: Creating an Altar for Hekate

Crafting an altar for Hekate is a profoundly intimate and spiritual encounter that is vital to any Hekatean ritual. An altar serves as a hallowed sanctuary where you can establish a profound bond with Hekate, pay homage to her, and seek her wisdom. Whether you are new to the realm of Modern Hekatean Witchcraft or a seasoned practitioner, crafting an altar dedicated to Hekate offers an exceptional opportunity to enrich your practice and form a closer connection with the Witchcraft Goddess.

Hekate is a powerful and enigmatic goddess known for her association with magic, witchcraft, crossroads, and liminality. As the mother of witchcraft, she is a guiding force for witches and magical practitioners worldwide. Creating an altar dedicated to her is a way to show your respect and devotion to this powerful deity. An altar for Hekate is not just a tool for witchcraft; it's also a place of power and transformation. It's a sacred space where you can communicate with the divine, seek guidance, and explore your spirituality. Whether you're seeking answers to life's big questions or working on manifesting your desires, an altar for Hekate can be an invaluable tool on your journey.

In this chapter, you'll explore the elements of creating an altar for Hekate, including the tools and symbols that are commonly used in Modern Hekatean Witchcraft. It'll also delve into the specifics of setting up your altar, including how to arrange your tools and offerings to reflect your personal witchcraft and devotion to the goddess. By the end of this chapter, you'll have all the knowledge and inspiration you need to create a personalized and powerful altar dedicated to the goddess of witches. It's time to connect with Hekate and let her guide you on your spiritual journey.

# Altar vs. Shrine

An altar is a space reserved for showcasing religious artifacts that hold significant meaning. The term "altar" is derived from "alter," which means to change. In Wicca, an altar may hold tools to practice their faith, such as an athame, deity representations, and items symbolizing the four elements or directions.

Nonetheless, the use of "altar" to describe a sanctified space displaying objects of worship for Hekate has been a matter of contention among her followers and practitioners of Hekatean witchcraft. Some argue that the appropriate term for this arrangement is a shrine, not an altar. If you intend to express devotion to Hekate, it's best to use the term *shrine* instead of *altar.* You can choose to merge both a shrine and an altar into a single sacred location if that resonates with you. Ultimately, it's your decision to determine the language that best suits your practice and feels right for you.

A shrine is a sacred space dedicated to expressing devotion and worship to a deity or spirit. It is a place where offerings are left, and prayers are said, a focal point for the expression of one's spiritual relationship with a particular being. In the case of Hekate, the goddess of witches, it is common for devotees to have a shrine in her honor. Shrines to Hekate often include images or representations of her and offerings such as candles, incense, and food. Keys are a common symbol associated with Hekate, representing her ability to unlock mysteries and open doors. Many devotees include keys on their shrines to express gratitude for Hekate's assistance in their lives.

Shrines can also serve as a place to petition Hekate for assistance or guidance. This can include placing offerings or items on the shrine that are infused with a specific intention or request, such as a photo of a loved one needing help. While a shrine is primarily a place of devotion and worship, it can also be used for divination practices. Many devotees use their shrines to communicate with the dead or receive messages from the goddess. Ultimately, the objects and offerings that one includes on their shrine should reflect their personal relationship with the goddess and their unique witchcraft practice. While common symbols and items are associated with Hekate, such as keys and portrayals of her, it is ultimately up to the individual to determine what they wish to include.

# Setting Up the Altar

When creating a shrine to honor Hekate, consider including a representation of her, such as a statue or picture. Many beautiful works of art are available, and if you choose to use artwork, make sure to buy a copy instead of just downloading and printing it. If you don't have the budget, look for public-domain images. Hekate, being the Queen of the Witches, appreciates having her own altar or altar space in a witch's home. In addition, you can also add items such as a cauldron, a knife, a broom, dog figurines, and decorations with stars and moons. It's important to cleanse and consecrate the space and tools in Hekate's name before setting them up, and then re-cleanse and charge them monthly on the Dark Moon. Remember that your shrine may start simple but will grow with time. Here are some guidelines you can keep in mind when setting up an altar for Hekate.

## 1. Choosing The Location

Choosing the right location for your altar is crucial to setting up a sacred space for Hekate. When deciding where to place your altar, consider factors such as privacy, accessibility, and atmosphere. You can choose a corner of your bedroom, a space on a bookshelf, or a small table in a quiet area of your home. The location you choose should be a place where you feel comfortable and safe, a place where you can focus your intention and energy.

When you're picking a spot, think about the energy of the space. Is it a place where you feel connected to nature or a place that feels dark and mysterious? Perhaps it's a space with a view of the night sky or a window that lets in natural light. Once you've chosen your spot, it's important to cleanse and consecrate it. You might use smoke from burning sage or incense to purify the space or sprinkle salt water to cleanse it. As you do that, call on Hekate to bless the area and protect it from negative energy.

## 2. When to Set It Up

When creating an altar for Hekate, timing can play an important role in building a stronger connection with this goddess. It's recommended to create the altar when the moon's energy is at its peak, such as on the night of the full moon, the new moon, or on a Monday. Here's why:

Firstly, the full moon is a time of heightened energy, abundance, and manifestation. It's a time when the moon is fully illuminated and radiating with powerful energy. Creating an altar for Hekate during the full moon can amplify your intentions and strengthen your bond with her, as the moon's energy will support your efforts. On the other hand, the new moon represents a time of new beginnings and fresh starts. It's a time for setting intentions and planting seeds for the future. By creating an altar for Hekate during the new moon, you'll tap into this energy and invite her to help you on your new journey.

Mondays are also a great time to create an altar for Hekate, as this day is associated with the moon and the goddess. Mondays are considered the best day for working with Hekate, as they provide an opportunity to start the week strong and focused. Creating an altar during these peak moon times can ensure that your intentions align with the moon's phases. This can provide a greater sense of harmony and balance in your life, which is key for any spiritual practice.

### 3. Keeping It Personal

When it comes to setting up a shrine to Hekate, it's important to keep it personal. While you can certainly purchase items to add to your shrine, creating your own objects can be one of the most meaningful ways to express devotion to Hekate. Don't worry if you don't consider yourself artistically inclined. The love and intention you put into the object matters most, not how great it looks on social media. However, if you're not inclined to create your own objects, that's perfectly fine too. What's important is that the objects you choose for your shrine are personal and reflect your feelings about Hekate.

Note that unlike in some Pagan traditions, Hekate does not reside in objects. Therefore, attempting to put her into an object is inappropriate. This would be considered blasphemy. Hekate is a powerful and multifaceted goddess who exists independently of any physical object. Therefore, when choosing objects for your shrine, it's important to remember that they are simply symbols of your relationship with her. Ultimately, the key to creating a personal shrine to Hekate is to let your intuition guide you. Choose objects that resonate with you and that you feel drawn to. Doing so will create a space uniquely your own and reflect the deep connection you share with this powerful and ancient goddess.

## 4. Hekate Colors

Hekate is often associated with specific colors that can be incorporated into her shrine. The colors most commonly associated with her are black, red, and white. These colors can be used in a variety of ways, from candles to fabric to cutouts made from paper. Black, in particular, is a color strongly associated with Hekate and can be used to represent the night, the unknown, and the mysteries of the underworld. Red is another color that is associated with Hekate, and it can be used to represent her power and passion. It can be used in candles, fabric, or other decorative items you may choose to include in your shrine. White, on the other hand, can be used to represent purity and clarity. It can be used as a background color for your shrine or as an accent color for decorative items.

Another color associated with Hekate is yellow or saffron. This color represents the harvest and the bountiful gifts of the earth. It can be used in fabric or in the form of decorative items like flowers or fruit. In addition to these colors, you may also want to consider the colors of objects associated with Hekate. For example, green is the color of oak trees, which are sacred to Hekate. You may want to include green in your shrine to represent the natural world and the power of the earth. Overall, using colors associated with Hekate is a great way to add depth and meaning to your shrine. By incorporating these colors in candles, fabric, or other decorative items, you can create a unique and personal space for your devotion to this powerful goddess.

## 5. Offerings

When it comes to offerings for a Hekate shrine, many traditional objects have been associated with Her throughout history. These can include things like garlic, saffron, oak leaves, and certain types of food. However, it's also important to consider personal objects that are significant to your devotion. For example, if you associate a particular flower with Hekate, you could include that in your shrine as an offering. Wild roses, which are associated with Hekate, are a great option for this. You can use them as permanent parts of the shrine or as offerings during the new moon phase. In addition to objects, you can also use symbols like dogs or snakes in your shrine. For example, having a statue of a dog or a snakeskin can be a great way to incorporate these symbols into your space.

Finally, it's worth noting that personal objects with symbolic meaning can be a powerful way to make offerings to Hekate. For example, you might include a piece of jewelry passed down to you by a family member or a small trinket that reminds you of a meaningful experience in your life. Whatever you choose, remember that the offering is meant to signify your devotion and appreciation for Hekate, so choose something that holds personal meaning for you.

## 6. Magical Tools and Sacred Objects

As a Modern Hekatean Witch, many sacred tools and magical objects can be used on your altar. These tools can help you connect with the energy of Hekate and aid in your magical workings. One of the most important things to keep in mind when choosing your tools is that they should be personal to you. You may want to consider making your own tools, as this can be a very meaningful way to express your devotion to Hekate.

Some examples of sacred tools that can be used on an altar include:

### 1. Knives and Blades

A knife is a common tool used in many magical traditions. It can be used for cutting herbs, carving symbols, and other practical purposes. Some witches use knives as offerings to Hekate, while others may use them for protection spells. As a Goddess associated with witchcraft and magic, Hekate is often linked to the use of knives and blades in rituals and spellwork. In Hecatean practice, knives and blades are considered sacred tools and are used to cut energy, cords, and other materials in spellwork.

Knives and blades are used for cutting cords, directing energy, and casting circles.
*Matus Kalisky, CC BY-NC-ND 2.0 DEED < https://creativecommons.org/licenses/by-nc-nd/2.0/>,*
*https://www.flickr.com/photos/31007239@N06/24477266240*

The athame, a double-edged knife, is common in Wiccan and Hekatean practice. It is used for casting circles, directing energy, and cutting cords. The athame is traditionally black-handled, symbolizing the element of fire, which represents will, passion, and transformation. To consecrate an athame for use in Hekatean practice, it can be cleansed with salt water, smudged with herbs like sage or mugwort, and charged under the full moon's light or in the presence of Hekate's image or statue.

Swords are also sometimes used in Hecatean practice, as they are associated with strength, protection, and the ability to cut through obstacles. They can be used to cast a circle or to symbolically cut ties with negative influences or situations. To consecrate a sword for Hecatean practice, it can be cleansed with salt water, smudged with herbs like frankincense or myrrh, and charged in the presence of Hekate's image or statue.

## 2. Candles

Candles are essential to many spiritual and magical practices, including Hekatean witchcraft. They can be used to represent the element of fire, which is associated with transformation, passion, and energy. In Hecatean altars, candles are often used to honor the goddess and bring the practitioner light and clarity.

**Candles are used to connect with Hekate.**
https://pixabay.com/es/photos/vela-la-magia-ritual-magia-4702150/

Hekate is often associated with fire, as she is considered a goddess of transformation and illumination. Candles are a great way to connect with Hekate and create a sacred atmosphere in her honor. They can be used in various ways, such as during meditation, ritual, or spell work. When choosing candles for a Hekatean altar, it is recommended to use black or red candles, colors associated with the goddess. You can also use white candles, which represent purity and clarity. You can use other colors, depending on the intention of the ritual or spell, such as green for abundance or blue for healing.

Before using the candles, consecrate them to Hekate. This can be done by holding the candle in your hands and focusing your intention on the goddess. You can also anoint the candle with oils, such as frankincense or myrrh, associated with Hekate. Once the candle is consecrated, it is ready to be used in ritual or spell work. When lighting the candles, saying a prayer or invocation to Hekate is customary. This can be as simple as calling out her name or reciting a longer invocation. The candles should be allowed to burn completely and should never be left unattended. As the candles burn, they serve as a reminder of the presence of Hekate and the power of transformation and illumination she brings.

### 3. Keys

In Hecatean practice, keys are a common sacred tool as they symbolize Hekate's role as the goddess of liminality and as the key-holder to the mysteries. Keys can be purchased or handmade and are typically displayed on the altar. They can be made of metal, wood, or other materials. To consecrate a key for use in a Hekatean altar, start by cleansing it with water, salt, or incense to remove any negative energies. Then, hold the key in your hands and visualize it being filled with Hekate's energy and power. You can also choose to say a prayer or invocation to Hekate, asking for her blessing and protection over the key.

**Keys are used as a symbol to unlock the mysteries of the universe.**
https://www.pexels.com/photo/two-black-skeleton-keys-on-an-old-paper-612800/

Keys can be used in various rituals and spells. For example, a key can open or close a ritual circle, symbolically unlock the mysteries of the universe, or invoke Hekate's guidance and protection. They can also be used in divination practices, such as scrying or tarot readings, as a symbol for unlocking hidden knowledge or secrets. When using a key in a ritual or spell, it is important to focus on its intention and ask for Hekate's guidance and blessings. After the ritual or spell is complete, the key should be returned to the altar and kept safely until its next use.

In addition to these traditional tools, many Modern Hekatean witches use talismans, knot spells, and other creative methods in their magical workings. These can include using cords, charms, markers, and paints to create personalized spells and offerings. The possibilities are endless, and your tools should be unique to your own practice and personal connection with Hekate.

Creating an altar for Hekate can be a deeply personal and rewarding practice. Remember that your altar reflects your devotion and commitment to Hekate, and it can evolve and change over time as you deepen your relationship with her. Don't be afraid to experiment and try new things, and always trust your intuition when designing your altar. Whether you're just starting out on your spiritual journey or you're a seasoned practitioner, building an altar for Hekate can be a powerful way to deepen your connection with the divine and access the transformative power of magic. So, go forth, gather your tools, and start creating a sacred space that honors the wisdom and magic of Hekate!

# Chapter 7: The Deipnon and Other Rituals

Ancient Greek magic was deeply intertwined with their religious beliefs, and their rituals and traditions were essential components of their daily lives. The Greeks believed in the existence of various gods and goddesses who were responsible for the different aspects of life. They believed these deities had the power to influence their lives, so they sought to appease them through various rituals and offerings.

One of the most important rituals in Ancient Greek magic was the Deipnon, held every month on the evening of the new moon. The Deipnon was a way for the Greeks to honor the goddess Hekate, the ruler of the underworld and the goddess of witchcraft, magic, and crossroads. The Greeks believed that Hekate had the power to grant them favors, protect them from evil spirits, and guide them through the dark of night.

During the Deipnon, offerings were made to Hekate and other gods and goddesses, including Zeus, Apollo, and Hermes. The offerings included libations, cakes, and incense, which were then left outside or on an altar. The Greeks believed that by making these offerings, they would gain the favor of the gods and receive their blessings.

The Deipnon was just one of many rituals that were an essential part of the Greek religious calendar. The Greeks celebrated various festivals and observances throughout the year, many linked to the seasons and the agricultural cycle. For example, Noumenia was a monthly observance held on the first day of the new moon, and it was a way for the Greeks to honor the god Apollo and ask for his blessings.

Another important ritual was the Home Blessing, performed annually to purify the home and ward off evil spirits. The Greeks believed that by performing this ritual, they would ensure the safety and prosperity of their household.

The Crossroads ritual was also an essential part of Ancient Greek magic. The Greeks believed that the crossroads were a place where the physical and spiritual worlds intersected; therefore, it was a place of great power. The Crossroads ritual was performed to invoke the aid of Hekate and other deities in matters related to magic and divination.

Ancient Greek magic was rich in ritualistic traditions and superstitions, and the Deipnon was just one of many important rituals performed to honor the gods and seek their favor. These rituals and beliefs were deeply intertwined with the Greek religious calendar and essential to their daily lives.

# Hekate Rituals

Hekate's protection rituals are steeped in mysticism and ancient religious practices, and though the specifics may have changed over time, the core remains the same. Hekate's protection rituals are designed to keep away evil and negative energies while inviting positive energy and blessings into your life. These rituals often involve burning incense, invoking the goddess's presence, and making offerings to her. While some of these rituals can be complex and require a great deal of preparation, others are relatively simple and straightforward. Regardless of the complexity of the ritual, Hekate's protection rituals offer a powerful way to protect yourself, your home, and your loved ones. They keep away negative energies while inviting positive energy and blessings into your life. In addition, honoring or calling on Hekate involves meditative qualities that bring peace and harmony and create a sense of safety and security. The rituals can even protect you from harm and give you the strength to face life's challenges. They can also create a more harmonious and peaceful atmosphere in your home and your relationships.

# Hekate's Deipnon

Hekate's Deipnon ritual is a mysterious and powerful ceremony shrouded in myth and speculation. Although the exact details of the ceremony remain unknown, what is known is that it was a monthly offering to

Hekate, made on the night of the new moon. It has been linked to many different spiritual and magical practices. While the exact details of the ritual are still largely unknown, scholars have been able to piece together some symbols and meanings associated with it. Most of the ritual pertains to offerings and prayers intended to honor the goddess and placate her anger. It is a practice still carried out today by devotees who seek to unlock the mysteries of this ancient ritual and gain access to Hekate's power and protection.

### Historical Practices

The ritual was performed at a crossroads, as these were believed sacred to Hekate and represented the point between the physical and spiritual worlds. Other locations included an altar or where air, water, and land met, such as on a bridge or a jutting rock. The ritual takes place on the darkest night of the year, usually around the end of the lunar month, which is thought to be a time of renewal and rebirth, and involves offerings of food and drink to the goddess. Participants in the ritual typically lit a candle and offered prayers and gifts to Hekate. The ritual was performed either as a solitary practice or with a group of like-minded individuals and was often accompanied by divination, with the purpose of seeking divine guidance and protection. It was believed to bring good luck and protection to the participant and their household. The ritual has three distinct parts.

- The first part was a meal consisting of food for the family and as an offering. Usually performed at a crossroads to honor the goddess and to thank her for her protection and guidance
- The second part of the ritual was the Expiation. This involved an animal sacrifice, such as a goat or a dog, to summon Hekate's benevolence
- The third part of the ritual was purification, which was performed to cleanse the home and ward off negative energies. This was typically carried out by burning incense, chanting prayers, and sprinkling holy water

The meal was the focal point of the ritual, with a variety of dishes such as fruits, vegetables, and grains being offered as a sign of respect. The family would take a few bites and offer the rest to the gods as a sign of respect. A typical Deipnon meal usually consisted of offerings of fish, honey, and sesame placed on the house's hearth. The meal was also shared with those who were not part of the family, including beggars and the poor, to commemorate the goddess' generosity.

All three portions of this ritual were an important part of honoring the goddess and receiving her blessings and was a time for reflection and contemplation. A time to reflect on one's spiritual journey and to ask for guidance and insight from Hekate. It was also an opportunity to let go of any pain, suffering, or negative emotions and commit to living a life of integrity and spiritual growth.

### Modern Day Practices

Nowadays, the Deipnon ritual is often practiced as a way to remember and honor family members who have passed away. People will gather with family and friends to share memories and stories of the deceased, share a meal, and light candles in their memory. The meal typically includes bread and salt, which symbolizes hospitality and protection. In some cultures, people may include a portion of the meal that the deceased enjoyed as a way to honor them.

Additionally, people will often share stories and memories of the deceased, allowing others to remember and honor their lives. This can be a very powerful and meaningful experience for those in mourning. Candles are lit in the deceased's honor, with each candle representing a different aspect of their life. This can include their spirit, their courage, their joy, or any other qualities that were special to them. After the candles are lit, the Deipnon ritual ends with a few moments of silence to reflect on and remember the person who has passed.

The Deipnon is also observed in a number of different ways. Some people may gather in a physical space to eat and offer prayers, while others may do so in their own homes or even online. Whatever the case, the intention is to honor and pay tribute to the gods and goddesses. It's also important to note that the Deipnon is not limited to any one religion or culture. People from many different religions and cultures observe the Deipnon in their own way, adapting it to their own practices.

# Noumenia (New Moon) Ritual

Unlike the Deipnon, which was celebrated on the last day of the month, the Noumenia ritual was celebrated with great enthusiasm on the first day of the new month. It was intended to bring the participants good luck, protection, and prosperity. It was a combination of magical practices and religious observances and was believed to be very powerful. A powerful form of divination, the Noumenia ritual was based on the movements of the stars and planets. Participants would study the heavens to determine the most auspicious times to perform the ritual. It was believed that the gods were watching the ritual and would intervene to ensure its success.

### Historical Practices

The ritual was usually held in a temple, at home in front of shrines, or outside under the glow of the moon, where the priestesses would conduct the ritual with offerings of grain, fruits, and flowers. After the ritual, the participants would enjoy a feast and exchange good wishes and tokens of appreciation. During the ritual, the participants would also make offerings and recite prayers to the gods and goddesses as a sign of their devotion. The ritual was also believed to be able to ward off bad luck and evil spirits. Participants would burn special incense, chant prayers, and make special offerings to the gods to protect them from any harm.

### Modern Day Practices

In modern times, this ritual has become a unique way to connect with the divine and observe the cyclical nature of the universe. It is a time of renewal, reflection, and connection with the spiritual realm. The contemporary practice of Noumenia involves setting aside time to connect with the divine, express gratitude, and focus on what one wants to manifest in the upcoming month. It is a time to take stock of the previous month and plan for the upcoming one. It is an opportunity to make a ritual out of the traditional practices of setting intentions, releasing anything that no longer serves you, and cultivating a sense of gratitude for the present moment. Typically, Noumenia is observed by creating a sacred space, lighting a candle, and connecting with the divine through prayer, meditation, or writing. One can also make offerings to their chosen deity, such as food, incense, or flowers. It is a time to express gratitude for all that has been received and to release any negativity experienced in the previous month.

# Home Blessing Ritual

The Hekate Home Blessing Ritual is a great way to bring positive energy and blessings into your home. This ancient ritual uses the power of the goddess Hekate to bring protection and blessings to your home and its inhabitants. The ritual itself is simple and straightforward.

1. Begin by lighting a white candle and placing it in the center of the room.

2. Visualize the white light of the candle radiating throughout the room.

3. As you do so, say a prayer to Hekate (anything you feel is appropriate), asking her to bring her power to your house.

4. Afterward, sprinkle some sea salt around the room, saying, *"May the protection of Hekate surround this room."*

5. Next, light some incense, saying, *"Hekate, bless my home with your protection and blessings."*

6. Allow the incense to burn for a few minutes, and then blow it out.

7. Finally, take some essential oil and anoint yourself, saying, *"Hekate, grant me protection and blessings."* You can also anoint the doorways and windows in your home.

# Crossroads (Transition/New Beginnings) Ritual

Difficult times can be a real challenge for many of us, and it's during these moments that Hekate's Crossroads can be a true source of strength and guidance. Hekate is the goddess of the crossroads. She holds the key, the flame, and the wheel, which allows her to provide insight and direction to those who seek it. The key to Hekate's crossroads is unlocking the potential within us. You use this key to unlock your deepest desires and dreams and explore the possibilities. The flame of Hekate's crossroads is the spark of inspiration that helps you to stay focused and motivated during difficult times. You can use this flame for kindling your passion and staying on course. The wheel of Hekate's crossroads serves as a reminder that life is full of cycles and that no matter how hard things may seem right now, they will eventually come to an end.

### Historical Practices

The Hekate crossroads ritual is an ancient form of witchcraft that has been around for centuries. It is believed to be a powerful form of magic that can significantly change one's life. This ritual is typically performed at a crossroads, which is considered a place of transition, transformation, and new beginnings. The practice involves the practitioner constructing a makeshift altar at the crossroads, upon which offerings such as coins, food, incense, and candles are placed. After making these offerings, the practitioner invokes Hekate and recites an invocation or prayer. This is then followed by a series of spells or chants meant to bring about the desired result. After the ritual, the practitioner leaves the crossroads, leaving the offerings behind, sometimes buried in the earth, as a thank you to Hekate. This practice was believed to bring luck, success, and protection from any negative energies encountered during the transition or new start. The Hekate crossroads ritual is believed to be incredibly powerful and should be used with caution.

### Modern Day Practices

The Hekate crossroads ritual is still practiced today, though it has evolved over time. Some practitioners opt to use modern symbols to honor Hekate, such as a candle or incense, and the ritual can be adapted to fit any personal needs. No matter how or where the ritual is conducted, it is still considered an effective way to honor Hekate and mark a transition to facilitate new beginnings. Modern-day rituals involve standing at whatever you use as your version of a crossroads, usually at midnight, and calling out to the Goddess Hekate three times. Offerings such as food, wine, incense, or coins can be made to help set the intention of the ritual. After the offerings are given, one should meditate and express their desire for a transition to Hekate. Following the meditation, it is important to thank the Goddess for her time and guidance. With the completion of this ritual, one should have the energy and clarity to make the changes necessary for a successful and prosperous change.

# Protection (Ghosts/Demon/Psychic Attacks) Ritual

The following Hekate protection ritual is designed to keep negative energies away and bring protection and blessings into your life. You can use it to ward off anything you believe brings bad energy into your life.

### Preparation

Before performing a Hekate protection ritual, it is important to prepare for the ritual. This includes cleansing and purifying the altar, gathering the necessary tools and items, and creating a sacred space.

1. Create a sacred space. This can be done by lighting candles, burning incense, and setting up an altar. The altar should be decorated with symbols of Hekate, such as a crescent moon or a triple goddess statue.
2. Cleanse and purify the altar. You can do this by smudging the altar with sage or other herbs or using salt and water to cleanse the area. This removes any negative energies that may be present and

creates a peaceful and sacred space.

3. Gather the necessary tools and items. This can include candles, incense, herbs, crystals, and offering bowls. It is also important to create an offering for Hekate, such as a small dish of honey, milk, or any other gift you feel is appropriate.

# Hekate Protection Rituals for Protection

The following Hekate protection ritual is designed to keep negative energies away and bring protection and blessings into your life.

1. First, light a white candle and place it on the altar

2. Then, light some incense and place it on the altar as well.

3. As the incense burns, recite the following invocation: *"Hekate, goddess of the night, Protect me from all that is not right. Keep away all evil, harm, and strife, and bring protection to my life."*

   *For protection for the home and family, recite the following: "Hekate, goddess of the night, Protect my home and family from all that is not right. Keep away all evil, harm, and strife, and bring protection and peace into our lives."*

4. Next, sprinkle salt around yourself and the altar to create a circle of protection.

5. Then, sprinkle some dried herbs around the altar, such as rosemary or lavender. As you do this, recite the following: *"Hekate, goddess of the night, Protect me and keep me from all that is not right. Bless me with protection and peace of mind and bring blessings to my life."*

6. Finally, make an offering to Hekate. This could be a small dish of honey or milk, or a few coins or other offerings. As you make the offering, recite the following: *"Hekate, goddess of the night, accept this offering as a sign of my gratitude. I thank you for your protection and blessings and for keeping me safe from all that is not right."*

   *For protection trials for the home and family, recite the following: "Hekate, goddess of the night, Accept this offering as a sign of my gratitude. I thank you for your protection and blessings and for keeping us safe from all that is not right."*

7. After completing the ritual, let the candle and incense burn until they are extinguished.

These rituals are often done in the dark of the night, as this is when the goddess is said to be most powerful.

As the goddess of witchcraft, crossroads, and the underworld, Hekate has been venerated in many forms and ways throughout the ages. Hekate rituals are typically focused on honoring the goddess and her qualities and gaining her favor and protection. Typically, these rituals involve offerings of food, incense, and other items that are sacred to her. These offerings can be placed at crossroads and other locations where she is said to dwell. Additionally, some practitioners perform invocations and spell to honor the goddess, and some even perform animal sacrifices to her. Hekate rituals are often celebrated on the night of the new moon, as this is said to be the time when the goddess is strongest and most powerful. Regardless of the ritual, the main theme is always reverence and respect for the goddess and her tremendous power.

# Chapter 8: Hekatean Spellwork

This chapter has spells that include prayers to Hekate, Hekatean herbs, plants, and oils, her symbols, and anything else that might associate with her. You can use these tools to draw on Hekate's power to protect your home, loved and yourself, getting advice in challenging situations or guidance through crossroads.

## Hekate Mojo Bag

Creating a Hekate mojo bag is one of the easiest ways to harness the goddess's protective powers and combine them with your own power. Once your pouch is done, you can carry or place it anywhere you want. For example, you can put it in your bag or pocket and bring it wherever you go. Anytime you feel the need for a little protective energy boost, you can take the pouch out, and you'll be reminded of the protection you have. Prepare this bag at night, preferably around the full moon.

### Ingredients:
- A small, mesh bag
- A piece of ribbon
- Small items collected from crossroads
- An obsidian
- A moonstone
- Lavender, dandelion, and cardamom (preferably in dried, lose form)
- A purple candle

**Instructions:**

1. Prepare your altar and tools by cleansing them with your favorite incense. This will also help you clear out your energy.

2. Light the candle, place all the ingredients into the mesh bag, and close it with the ribbon.

3. Keep the pouch in your hands for 10 minutes to imbue it with your energy. While charging the bag, you can reach out to Hekate and ask her to add her power to it. Say this when calling on Hekate:

   *"Hekate, you who are on both sides and in between,*

   *You who reside in the crossroads, who guard the threshold,*

   *I implore you to protect me.*

   *Grant me safe passage as I navigate through life.*

   *Protect me in every new space and from negative spirits*

   *Protect me forces lurking in the in-between spaces*

   *Hekate, hear my prayer!"*

4. When you feel ready, snuff out the candle and place the pouch where you intend to use it. From time to time, you'll need to recharge it with your energy and that of the goddess to keep its powers.

# Hekate Essential Oil Blend

This essential oil blend can be used for several purposes, including protection, spiritual communication, and pathway clearing. You can apply it to candles and other items you want to infuse with the goddess's power or use it in spells when working with Hekate. Prepare the oil blend on the night of the full moon, and let it charge until the dark phase of the moon.

**Ingredients:**

- Poppy
- Lavender
- Mayapple
- Mugwort
- Dirt for a crossroads
- Garlic
- Hair from a dog (preferably black)

- A bottle
- Olive oil or walnut oil

**Instructions:**

1. Working under the full moon (outside or near a window), mix all the ingredients (except the oil).

2. Pour the mixture into a bottle, and fill the leftover space with the oil

3. Leave the bottle outside or on the windowsill to soak in the moonlight and the goddess's energy.

4. When it's charged, carry it over to your altar and leave it there until the dark moon. Shake it from time to time to imbue it with your energy.

# Home Protection Blend

With this herbal blend, you can invoke Hekate's power as the protector, averter of hostile forces, and the protector of crossroads and thresholds. It uses herbs associated with the goddess and salts that also contribute to the protection of your home. You can sprinkle them near windows and doors or at a threshold shrine that protects your home from the inside out. This will only require you to place the image or symbols of the goddess on a shelf near the entrances. If you opt for this method, leave small offerings as well (even if you can only offer spiritual messages).

**Ingredients:**

- A sprinkle of poppy powder to confuse malicious spirits
- A sprinkle of garlic powder for protection
- A sprinkle of white sage powder for good luck
- A small handful of dirt from the crossroads or brick dust
- A charcoal disk
- The representation of the goddess
- A purple candle

**Instructions:**

1. Mix the herbs together in a small bowl. Use a little of their herbs (together with essential oils) for anointing the purple candle. This adds another layer of protection to your home. When doing this, say the following:

*"Hekate, I light this candle in your honor.*

*Just as its flame burns bright, so may your torches burn and guide me eternally.*

*I ask you to look upon my home as I am your devoted follower.*

*Grant me this favor and protect my home from harm and mishap."*

2. Pour some of the dried herbal mixtures onto the charcoal disk and burn it while reciting the following prayer:

   *"Goddess Hekate, I invoke you as I burn these herbs for you. I ask you to bless them as they are from your sacred garden.*

   *Lend them your protection and grant me your blessing.*

   *I implore you to imbue the rest of the herbs with enough resilience to protect my home."*

3. Combine the herbs with the dirt or brick powder. Let the purple candle burn down completely, but don't leave it unattended. You can do this throughout several nights during the dark phase of the moon.

4. When the candle has completely melted, gather the wax, and put it in a small pouch. You can use this as a charm by hanging it up near the entrance, next to the small altar on the shelf. Alternatively, you can bury the pouch outside your home on your property.

5. Give offerings to the goddess at your altar. Then, carry the herbs to the altar at the entrance of your home and sprinkle them across the thresholds. Or, disperse them around all the entry points (including all windows and doors). When doing this, address Hekate with the following prayer:

   *"Hekate, as I stand before this threshold, I place these herbs before you and ask for your guidance and protection.*

   *Please protect my home and those living in it.*

   *May all the negative energies be kept away, and may your power bless this place.*

   *May my entrances always be protected by you,*

   *and may you never cease to shield me from malicious influences.*

   *Hekate, avert any misfortune and watch over me as your devoted follower.*

*Grant me this favor so I may have safe shelter."*

6. Now, you'll have a powerful significant barrier protecting your home and those living there.

7. You can repeat the spell regularly as needed, although some recommend doing this once a year. However, occasionally recharging your herbal blend will allow you to keep the protection longer without redoing it.

8. Every time you cross the entrance, say a quick prayer of appreciation to Hekate. If you have a small altar near the main entrance, do it there. With each word of gratitude, you're building your connection to the goddess, and she will be more inclined to help you out.

# Keybearer Spell

Using old keys as protective charms, you can draw on Hekate's power to find guidance, and protection, open new paths, or have questions answered. For example, suppose you put a key under your pillow after this keybearer spell. In that case, you can communicate with Hekate in your dreams. You can hang the keys above your altar, place them on top, or wear them on a necklace as a good luck charm. You can also use spells designed to find a lost object or unlock secrets and lock your home in a protective layer.

### Ingredients:
- A key
- A small box with a latch
- A black candle
- Other candles associated with your intention
- Rosemary, sage, and lavender in dried, loose form
- Paper and pen
- Incense of your choice

### Instructions:
1. Gather your supplies during a waxing or full moon phase - the latter will give you full potency.
2. Purify your space and tools by smudging, placing them in salt, or whatever cleansing method you prefer.

3. Light the candles associated with your purpose and the incense, and turn down any artificial lights.

4. Light the black candle and say:

*"I call on Hekate, the Keybearer, to fill this candle flame with her ancient wisdom and magical essence.*

*May it empower my spell for protection."*

5. Take a piece of paper, and write down your clear intention (focusing on what you want to protect, unlock, or hide) and the paper several times towards you.

6. Put the paper in the box and sprinkle the herbs over it while asking each to enact their powers. Close the box and visualize how you manifest your intent. For example, if you want to unlock secrets in your dreams, picture yourself lying down on the bed and speaking with Hekate in your dreams.

7. Take your key, and holding it above the candle flame, say:

*"May this key ward off evil and negative influences."*

*I bear the key now, and I shall unlock its power."*

8. Place the key under your pillow to find answers in your dreams. Go to bed and wait for your answers. When you receive them, write them down as soon as you wake up.

9. You can unlock the box and release the spell when you get your answers.

# Strophalos Crystal Grid

Crystal grids are great for concentrating and combining the strengths of the individual stones. Using a Strophalos crystal grid lets you draw on Hekate's power to protect your home. You can set it up near a window and channel its energy outside the house with the goddess's help. It's recommended to do this during the darkest phase of the moon when the moon's liminal power is the strongest. This way, the grid protects your home for all spirits – from this world, the underworld, and those residing in between.

### Ingredients:

- A Strophalos (Hekate's Wheel grid mat - you can draw a grid on a piece of cloth on your own or buy one premade)

- Stones associated with Hekate (jade, obsidian, ruby, sapphire, pearl, jasper, moonstone)
- Other stones you feel drawn to
- A large bowl
- Candles

**Instructions:**

1. Start by cleansing and charging the stones. The most effective way to do this is to place them in a bowl and leave them on a windowsill for at least one night during the waning phase of the moon.

2. Set your intentions by visualizing, journaling, or otherwise bringing your desire into focus. Use present tense and a positive tone. For example, instead of saying: *"I don't want my home to be defenseless,"* say: *"My home is protected."*

3. Clean the place where you want to keep your grid from clutter, and use smudging to banish harmful energies. Slowly carry your smudging stick around your home to make sure that the negative energy is eliminated from every corner.

4. Place the cloth with the grid on the designated space. Focusing on your intention, begin placing the crystals around the pattern. Keep each stone in your hands for a few seconds to infuse them with your energy.

5. If you have trouble concentrating, start by putting the first crystal in the middle to center you and the energy of the crystals. This first crystal should correspond to the fundamental purpose of your grid. For Hekate's protection, place obsidian in the middle. Putting a piece of paper with your intention or a symbol attached to it also helps focus the grid's energy.

6. Place the remaining crystals around the middle one. When you're finished, move on to charging your grid. You can do this by meditating on your intent or through any other means that help you connect with your magical tools.

7. Once your intentions are set, you can dismantle the grid or leave it as it is until you start to see the effects. If you keep it, make sure to revisit it each night and say a prayer to Hekate.

# Strophalos Necklace Charm

This necklace charm has one of the ancient symbols associated with the goddess - Hekate's wheel. Also called the symbol of the triple goddess, this tool can be a powerful ally for psychic protection. By charging it, you can empower it with Hekate's energy, while wearing it will ensure that the charms stay in contact with your energy. If you feel that you're being influenced by negative psychic energy, touch your pendant to remind yourself that you have the power to ward off negative influences.

### Ingredients:

- A necklace with a pendant depicting Hekate's wheel
- Salt - in a little bowl
- Incense
- 1 Moonstone
- 1 Obsidian
- Jasper
- A black candle
- Representations of the goddess, such as keys, symbols of her animals, or death

### Instructions:

1. Place your ingredients on your altar at dusk during the full moon phase. Keep your window open to let the moonlight in.

2. Place the pendant and the necklace into the bowl of salt. You can move the windowsill under the moonlight for a few minutes to charge it with the goddess's power.

3. For the best results, prepare yourself by taking a cleansing bath while your jewelry is cleansed and charged.

4. When you're done with your bath, light the candle and place it in the middle of the altar. Put the representation of the goddess next to the candle.

5. Place the three stones in front of you on the altar in a semicircle. Take out the jewelry from the bowl and place it in front of the stones.

6. Call on Hekate with the following prayer:

   *"Hekate, I ask you to hear my prayers!*

*I call upon you to protect me from evil spirits.*

*Shield me from those who do not rest but roam the world, wanting to cause harm.*

*You who rule those spirits less than god, please withdraw them from my presence.*

*Hekate, Gate-Keeper of the Crossroads, protect my psyche from negative energies and banish malevolence from my presence!"*

7.  Take the charm into your hands and feel its warm, protective energy. Place it around your neck, and wear it to remain protected from malevolent spiritual energies.

# Hekate's Open Pathway Spell

This spell can invoke Hekate, whether you want to work with her as the Torch Bearer, the Keeper of Keys, or the. You can use it to cleanse your path from negative influences, uncover new opportunities, or find the road to a successful life. The spell incorporates several items associated with Hekate, including herbs and symbols of the animals.

## Ingredients:

- Keys and other symbols of Hekate
- 3 orange candles
- Lavender essential oil
- A mixture of sage, cinnamon, lavender, dandelion root, and frankincense
- Dirt from a crossroads
- Incense of your choice (sage is best for cleansing and protection)
- Offerings for Hekate (food, art, or whatever you wish to gift)

## Instructions:

1.  At night, during the darkest phase of the moon, prepare your tools by placing them on your altar. Start by adorning the space with symbols you use for representing the goddess (minus one key).
2.  Light your incense and focus on your intention.
3.  Anoint the three candles in lavender essential oil and the herbal mixture. The sacred herbs of Hekate will provide guidance, cleansing, and success in your magical pursuit.

4. Place the candles in the middle of the altar in an inverted triangle. Sprinkle the crossroad dirt and more loose herbs around the candles. When sprinkling the herbs, make a line between each candle.

5. Put a key between the three candles, and make an offering to the goddess. Then start reciting the following prayer while lighting the first candle:

   *"Hekate, Guardian of the Crossroads, I seek you.*

   *I ask you to open my paths and cleanse them of energetic blockages, misfortune,*

   *and anything that would steer me from my path."*

6. Lighting the second candle, chant:

   *"Hekate, shine your bright lights upon my path to prosperity.*

   *Torch Bearer, steer me away from misguided paths.*

   *May your flames burn eternal and illuminate my road to success."*

7. Lighting the third candle, say:

   *"Keeper of the Keys, open the doors to a journey that leads to new opportunities and victory.*

   *Hekate, I ask you to Bless me with luck, good fortune, and the key to triumph.*

   *You who are found in every crossroads, help me avoid closed doors."*

8. Take a deep breath, sit back, and continue with your prayer:

   *"Hekate, Patron of all Witches, listen to my prayers. As I light these candles, may their flame bestow me power as potent as the fire of your torches.*

   *Clear my ways on this journey, and show me the way to unlock the best opportunities. Goddess Hekate, I implore you to empower this spell with all your divine essence."*

9. Let the candle burn all the way down, but don't leave them unattended. You can relight them as many times as it takes them to burn down. When they're finished, dispose of the wax at a crossroads.

10. Carry the key from the spell as a charm. When you receive the blessing you asked for, make another offering to express your gratitude to Hekate.

# Chapter 9: Divination with Hekate

Divination is the practice of predicting the future by interpreting signs, omens, and messages in nature. It is an ancient form of foretelling used throughout history to seek insight into relationships, finances, health, and more. Divination serves as a way for individuals to understand what lies ahead or to receive guidance about their current situation or course of action.

This practice can help you make sense of your life and gain clarity about what may be in store for you in the future. Seeking guidance from divination practices can increase your knowledge and understanding of past events, enabling you to plan for the future with greater insight. By tapping into this guide, you can also gain greater self-awareness and become more attuned to any energies or situations that may be hindering your progress.

Moreover, divination allows you to understand yourself better and reveals your hidden gifts and talents. It also provides access to spiritual knowledge that may not be readily available through other means. Making decisions based on a higher level of understanding than just gut instinct alone allows you to tap into your inner wisdom, which can guide you on how best to respond when faced with challenging situations. Additionally, divinatory practices can guide you toward taking the necessary steps for personal growth, thereby enabling you to reach your goals faster and more effectively.

Using divination can foster a deeper connection between you and the divine, revealing deeper truths about yourself and offering practical daily life advice that promotes physical wellness and emotional balance. Through these readings, you can better understand yourself on a deeper level, leaving room for meaningful change within your life.

# Goddess Hekate's Role in Divination

Goddess Hekate has long been associated with divination and prophecy. In ancient Greek mythology, Hekate was often portrayed as a powerful Goddess of supernatural knowledge, linking the mortal world with the divine realms. She was the goddess of the crossroads, and her presence in those places allowed her to be seen as a bringer of messages from the future. She is also associated with dark magic and necromancy, making her an ideal figure for divination rituals.

In many cultures, Hekate is seen as a guardian of doorways between worlds, and this connection to travel makes it easy to see how she became tied to divination. For instance, tarot cards are tools Hekate used to travel through space and time, allowing her to communicate more effectively with mortals in the present day. These cards allow one to access past events or gain information about future events. Additionally, Hekate is often associated with astrology and lunar cycles. Ancient Greeks would consult her prior to embarking on any journey or making major decisions in life as she was believed to offer insight into what was ahead.

Hekate's association with necromancy also ties into divination. Communicating with the dead can provide insights into unknowns in the living world. This could take many forms. One could use mediums or seers who specialized in interpreting signs from beyond, consulting occult texts for advice about life and death, or even engaging in trance-like states where visions from beyond could be revealed. All these methods combined (tarot cards, astrology/lunar cycles & necromancy) allowed Hekate to provide devotees seeking knowledge - both mundane & spiritual - a way to access deeper layers of insight that allowed them to make informed decisions based on a more holistic approach than relying solely on physical evidence alone.

# Divination Arts Associated with Hekate

### 1. Crystal Ball Scrying

Crystal ball scrying is an ancient form of divination that involves looking into an orb-shaped object, such as a crystal ball or reflective surface, to receive insights and messages from the spiritual realm. This practice is believed to be centuries old and has frequently been used by mystics and psychics alike to invoke visions of the future. It can also be used to gain a greater understanding of one's personal life experiences. During crystal ball scrying, the practitioner focuses their gaze deeply into the sphere while breathing deeply in an effort to reach a meditative state. Once these methods have been accomplished, images may appear within the crystal ball that is then interpreted according to the individual's beliefs and knowledge of symbolism. When interpreting these images, practitioners need to remain open-minded and non-judgmental in order for them to gain deeper insight into what they are seeing. In addition to receiving prophetic messages, those who engage with this practice often report feeling peacefulness, clarity of mind, and higher levels of intuition.

Crystal ball scrying can be enhanced with Hekatean magic, as it is rooted in the same spiritual energy of the goddess Hekate.

Hekatean magic can be incorporated into crystal ball scrying by first preparing the space, setting up your altar, and gathering supplies like incense, candles, herbs, stones, or tarot cards corresponding to the goddess's energies. An altar with images of Hekate should also be present, along with other items that represent her domains, such as keys, coins, and herbs. Candles in shades of purple, black, silver, or white should be lit around the area as symbols of Hekate's presence. Incense of myrrh or frankincense can also be used to increase the energies surrounding the ritual space. Then, you should offer a prayer or invocation to invoke her spirit into the room and allow her energy to infuse your practice.

When ready, an invocation of Hekate should be spoken or sung aloud to call upon her guidance and power. This invocation should express gratitude for her presence and ask for protection from dangers that may arise during the scrying session. Once this invocation is complete, one can move on to gazing into their crystal ball to receive messages from spirit realms beyond our own.

Once the space is prepared and blessed, it's time to begin scrying with the crystal ball. Begin by holding the ball in both hands while focusing on Hekate's energy and asking for guidance. Asking questions silently within yourself will bring forth psychic visions from within the depths of the crystal ball. Focus your vision on the depths of the sphere as if looking through a window into another realm, allowing images and symbols to appear before your inner eye to provide insight into the question asked.

The energies that flow through the crystal ball can be used to help interpret these visions. For example, if you see symbols related to protection or guardianship during scrying, you may want to consider how this ties into Hekate's protective energy and reflect on what it means for your life. While looking into the crystal ball, it is important to remain open and relaxed to best receive information from these unseen realms through visual images or thoughts that come up from within oneself or from outside sources. Additionally, using tarot cards with the same themes as Hekate's realm - like death and rebirth, crossing boundaries, or navigating darkness - can further enhance your divination practice by providing a more in-depth interpretation of the messages from the crystal ball.

When your scrying session has ended, thank Hekate for her guidance before releasing her energy from the room. You can use another prayer or invocation, and the ritual should end with extinguishing any candles or incense that have been used.

Combining crystal ball scrying with Hekatean magic makes it possible to reach a deeper understanding of one's life path and gain insight into the mysteries of the world around you. As an ancient goddess who has long been associated with portals between realms, Hekate's energies are invaluable when exploring the unknown through divination. By inviting her spirit into your practice, you will be able to access powerful guidance from beyond our physical realm and make use of her magic in a safe and informed way.

By incorporating Hekate into crystal ball scrying, great insights can be obtained by connecting with her immense energy. She will use her dominion over magic and mysticism to assist you properly when you call upon her. When done properly, crystal ball scrying is a powerful practice that can allow for exploration beyond the physical realm. Hekate will guide you on your path if you are willing to reach out for her help.

## 2. Black Mirror Scrying

Black mirror scrying is an ancient divinatory psychic practice whereby one peers into a surface, usually a black or dark-colored mirror, for insight, reflection, and connection. It has been used since antiquity to connect with the spiritual world and reveal hidden knowledge. The only real tools needed are a still and dark room, a black mirror made of obsidian or hematite, or an empty bowl or container filled with still water. This process encourages enhanced intuition and allows a person to probe deeper into their subconscious mind to gain insight into situations or better understand oneself.

When practicing black mirror scrying, Hekate's presence can be invoked to aid in connecting with the spirit world and gaining insight from beyond the veil of death. To effectively use this magic, it's important to understand the relationship between you and Hekate. She can serve as both a guide and protector, offering her wisdom when called upon for assistance. However, showing respect and avoiding demanding or disrespectful requests is crucial, as Hekate will only respond in kind.

To incorporate Hecatean magic into your black mirror scrying, the first step is to create an altar or sacred space for your ritual work. This space should include items representing the goddess and her power, such as a statue or figurine, candles, incense, and other meaningful objects. Meditating on these objects can help you establish a connection with Hekate and open yourself up to her influence. It's also important to use protective energy when invoking the goddess, such as by drawing a circle around yourself with salt to create a boundary between you and any negative entities present during the ritual.

In addition to setting up a sacred space, you can use symbols associated with Hekate during the black mirror scrying ritual. For example, a triskele, a three-legged wheel, can represent knowledge gained through journeys between worlds, symbolizing the process of crossing over into non-physical realms via black mirror scrying. You can draw a representation of the triskele on the surface of the black mirror or place it nearby during the ritual. Additionally, you can incorporate various plants associated with Hekate, such as mugwort and mandrake root, known for their ability to bring forth prophetic visions during divinatory practices. Adding these plants either directly onto the surface of the black mirror or placing them near it can enhance its power when used within this type of ceremonial work dedicated to Hekate's patronage.

Besides using visual symbols associated with Hekate, verbal invocations could also be used during a black mirror scrying ritual while asking for guidance from beyond this realm. These should include requests for personal insight and protection while engaging in divination activities such as those involving mirrors. Invocations could take many forms, including spoken word prayers and poem recitations, allowing participants to shape their personal connection with Hekate according to their needs and intentions for that particular session.

Once you have created your altar and established a connection with Hekate, you are ready to begin scrying with the black mirror. Focus your attention on the dark surface of the mirror and allow yourself to go into a meditative state. While visualizing Hekate in her three-headed form, ask her for assistance and guidance to understand what lies beyond the mirror's surface. At this point, many practitioners like to perform a guided visualization exercise or explore their own minds in an effort to uncover hidden knowledge or visions that may appear in the reflection of the black mirror. As you look into its depths, take note of any images, symbols, or words that come to mind, as this can provide valuable insight into your spiritual understanding and personal growth.

Once you feel you have explored your inner thoughts and any visions that may appear in the mirror, thank Hekate for her help before ending the ritual.

Hekatean magic and black mirror scrying can be an incredibly powerful combination when practiced responsibly and with respect for the goddess' power. With their combined forces, one can uncover inner truths and gain insight into what lies ahead, allowing them to make choices based on knowledge rather than fear or uncertainty.

By incorporating Hekatean magic in black mirror scrying, one can open themselves up to a new realm of spiritual exploration and gain insight into their past life, current situation, and future possibilities. When used correctly, this powerful magic can reveal hidden truths about oneself and help guide them on their journey toward personal growth and enlightenment. With practice and dedication, anyone can use these ancient techniques to explore their own power and deepen their connection with the divine.

### 3. Tarot/Oracle Cards

If you're interested in divination, you may have heard of oracle and tarot cards as popular tools for gaining insight and guidance. Tarot cards, consisting of 78 cards, often incorporate astrological symbols, archetypes, and numerology. The interpretation of these cards relies on the reader's intuition and the symbolism developed over the centuries. On the other hand, oracle cards are simpler in design and usually have 25-40 individual cards that can be used alone or combined with other decks, and the reader's intuition also interprets the meanings. People around the world have used these tools for centuries to access higher wisdom and gain insight into various issues.

If you practice Hekatean magic and are interested in using tarot or oracle cards, you can incorporate Hekate's energy into your readings. For instance, you could use imagery depicting Hekate, such as her classical Greco-Roman form with three heads, on the face of the cards. Alternatively, you could use symbols associated with Hekate, such as keys, torches, snakes, or dogs, to evoke her presence within the deck. With an offering of prayer or ritualistic elements, you can connect with her energy to gain clarity on the issues you're facing.

Additionally, you could incorporate themes closely linked to Hekate's energy, such as cycles. The major arcana cards could represent the cycles of life, death, and rebirth with which Hekate has traditionally been associated. Imagery, such as a snake eating its own tail, or symbols, such as a wheel or spiral, could be used to convey these themes in the readings. Many practitioners of Hekatean witchcraft view tarot cards as vessels that may be used to invoke spiritual guidance from the patron Goddess herself.

Using tarot or oracle cards in combination with Hekatean magic can be a powerful tool for gaining insight and guidance in your spiritual practice. By incorporating Hekate's energy and themes into your readings, you can deepen your connection to her and better understand the issues you're facing.

Hekate also has a strong connection to the moon – especially the new/dark/waning moons – so incorporating this element into Oracle cards would effectively invoke her presence. The card images themselves could involve depictions of crescent moons, stars, wolves howling at the moon, and other symbolic items associated with the lunar cycle. Similarly, Hekate's connection to crossroads and liminal spaces could be explored within Tarot readings using visual motifs such as two roads meeting in the middle of nowhere or a character standing at the edge of a cliff.

In addition to visual elements, her presence could also be invoked through words and phrases – either printed on the cards or used during readings. For example, keywords associated with Hekate, such as "liminal," "cycle," "pathway," or "journey," can invoke her energy. Similarly, affirmations such as "I am present at this moment" could also be included on the face of Oracle cards as a way to remind readers that they are not alone in their journey and that Hekate is there to offer guidance.

Hekatean magic can be incorporated into the structure of Tarot/Oracle readings themselves. Generally speaking, most decks incorporate three-card spreads – each card representing a past, present, and future element. This could be expanded upon to represent the three faces of Hekate in reading. For example, one card could represent her Maiden aspect (past), another card could represent her Mother aspect (present), and the third card could represent her Crone aspect (future). Alternatively, a nine-card spread can also be used to represent Hekate's role as a triple Goddess. In this case, each set of three cards is assigned its own theme or focus area; for example, one set could focus on healing while another set could focus on transformation.

Incorporating Hekatean magic into Tarot/Oracle decks can be a great way to enhance the reading experience and invoke her energy in everyday life. Through visual motifs, words/phrases, and unique spread structures, readers can access Hekate's wisdom interactively and creatively that is still rooted in traditional witchcraft practices.

### 4. Bone Casting

Hekatean magic can be incorporated into bone casting, also known as scapulimancy. Bone casting divination involves taking a set of animal bones and creating a cast from them to look for patterns that offer insight into the future or answers to questions asked by the ritual participant. Hekate can be invoked in this ritual in several ways. Hekatean bone casting is a specific type of bone divination in which the practitioner uses talismans associated with Hekate, such as crayfish claws, vulture feathers, and mandrake root, to cast bones to glimpse what lies ahead.

Before beginning any magical work, having a proper mindset and focusing your intentions on what you want to gain from experience is important. For Hekatean bone casting, light a candle or incense dedicated to Hekate and say an invocation or prayer asking for her assistance in your divination. During the bone-casting divination ritual, incense offerings are often made to honor Hekate and invite her protection while engaging with spiritual forces. The type of incense used is usually based around herbs sacred to Hekate, such as juniper or cypress, which are believed to bring her closer. Many practitioners will draw a pentacle on the ground before beginning the ritual, invoking Hekate's presence in it. Alternatively, an icon or statue of Hekate can be placed nearby as an offering and symbol of her presence.

After establishing this connection with the goddess, pick out a set of bones you feel drawn to. The type of bone used will vary depending on the practitioner. Once you have picked out your preferred set of bones, cleanse them in a mixture of rosemary and sea salt water before drying them off and charging them with energy through meditation.

Once the bones are charged and ready to be used, it is time to begin casting them. Start by spreading a white cloth on the floor with your chosen set of bones placed in the center. Place both of your hands over the bones, focusing your intentions on what you want to learn from them. Begin slowly rolling the bones around while asking a specific question or focusing on an area of life you want insight into. As you roll the bones, pay close attention to how they interact with each other and if any patterns emerge between them as they move across the cloth. Each bone will have its own significance, so take note of which ones are being rolled together more than others and use intuition to make interpretations.

After completing the bone cast and looking for any patterns that may appear within it, practitioners can choose to ask for further guidance from Hekate by meditating on her iconography or drawing additional symbols connected to her, such as stars or keys. Additionally, you can offer prayers to ask for guidance from her on how best to interpret what was received through the bone-casting reading.

Once you know what the bones might be telling you, take some time to reflect on their messages and consider how they could relate to your current situation or future path. Finally, after receiving any insights gained through this process, it is customary to thank Hekate for her assistance and make offerings once more in gratitude, either verbally or with further incense burning.

Hekatean bone casting is a powerful divination practice that can provide practitioners with valuable insights into both their present and future. By connecting with the goddess Hekate and using intuition while interpreting the messages of the bones, practitioners can better understand their lives and make informed decisions based on the information they receive.

# Bonus: Orphic Hymn to Hekate

**Translated Text:**

*"I call Hekate of the Crossroads, worshipped at the meeting of three paths, oh lovely one.*

*In the sky, earth, and sea, you are venerated in your saffron-colored robes.*

*Funereal Daimôn, celebrating among the souls of those who have passed.*

*Persian, fond of deserted places, you delight in deer.*

*Goddess of night, protectress of dogs, invincible Queen.*

*Drawn by a yoke of bulls, you are the queen who holds the keys to all the Kózmos.*

*Commander, Nýmphi, nurturer of children, you who haunt the mountains.*

*Pray, Maiden, attend our hallowed rituals;*

*Be forever gracious to your mystic herdsman and rejoice in our gifts of incense."*

### Original Greek Text:

*"Εἰνοδίην Ἑκάτην κλήιζω, τριοδῖτιν, ἐραννήν,*

*οὐρανίην, χθονίαν τε, καὶ εἰναλίην κροκόπεπλον,*

*τυμβιδίην, ψυχαῖς νεκύων μέτα βακχεύουσαν,*

*Πέρσειαν, φιλέρημον, ἀγαλλομένην ἐλάφοισιν,*

---

νυκτερίην, σκυλακῖτιν, ἀμαιμάκετον βασίλειαν,
ταυροπόλον, παντὸς κόσμου κληιδοῦχον ἄνασσαν,
ἡγεμόνην, νύμφην, κουροτρόφον, οὐρεσιφοῖτιν,
λισσόμενοις κούρην τελεταῖς ὁσίαισι παρεῖναι
βουκόλῳ εὐμενέουσαν ἀεὶ κεχαρηότι θυμῷ."

# Conclusion

The goddess Hekate is known for having both good and evil sides. She is the deity of witchcraft, doorways, magic, the moon, necromancy, and creatures associated with nighttime. Hekate's immense power is undeniable, which is why some people associate her with dark power and evil. That said, most people regard her as the deity of protection and guidance. She is often depicted as a beautiful woman holding a torch, signifying her association with darkness and the night. She is also usually depicted with three faces, symbolizing her role as the deity of crossroads and her ability to look and watch over all directions.

Even though she is a widely popular figure in Greek mythology and in the world of witchcraft, she was never initially a member of the Greek pantheon. Like the deities Dionysus and Demeter, Hekate originated in ancient Thrace, which predates ancient Greece. Originally, the goddess was believed to rule over the seas, heavens, and Earth. All deities, including Zeus, the king of the Greek gods, honored Hekate. She was also the only deity at the time to retain her powers after siding with the Olympians to defeat the Titans.

Over time, Hekate's power became more defined, shaping her as the protector goddess of witches, magic, and crossroads we know today. Neopagans regard her as a prominent symbol of their practices and an archetype among the deities. Wiccans, to this day, worship her as the goddess of magic, darkness, and the moon.

Now that you have read this book, you know everything you need to know about Hekate. Learning about her history, stories, how she manifests herself, and what she means to different people can help you work with her more effectively. Knowing all the symbols and tools associated with the goddess will allow you to build the perfect altar and give you ideas about which items to incorporate into your daily life. Making aspects of Hekate a constant part of your life can help you strengthen your relationship with her.

Learning which offerings to give Hekate shows her how much you respect and appreciate her. Giving the deities meaningful offerings is key to building relationships with them. Not all deities prefer the same offerings- what is significant for one deity might be disrespectful to another. This is why you should check which offerings are appropriate to give Hekate once you set up her altar.

After reading this ultimate guide to understanding Hekate, you should've gained insight into how you relate to Hekate and determined the best way to go about your practice. Now that you're ready to start working with the goddess, you can always return to this book for guidance. While you might need the guidance of an experienced practitioner if you want to delve deeper, this book can help you grasp the basics you need to go further on your journey with Hekate.

# Here's another book by Mari Silva that you might like

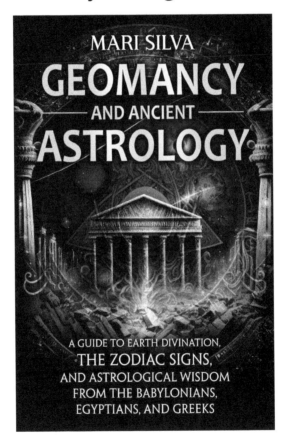

# Your Free Gift
# (only available for a limited time)

Thanks for getting this book! If you want to learn more about various spirituality topics, then join Mari Silva's community and get a free guided meditation MP3 for awakening your third eye. This guided meditation mp3 is designed to open and strengthen ones third eye so you can experience a higher state of consciousness. Simply visit the link below the image to get started.

https://spiritualityspot.com/meditation

**Or, Scan the QR code!**

# References

(N.d.). Umich.edu. http://websites.umich.edu/~umfandsf/symbolismproject/symbolism.html/L/ladder.html#:~:text=The%20ladder%20(or%20staircase)%20is,on%20the%20ladder%20of%20virtue.

(N.d.). Usnews.com. https://www.usnews.com/news/best-countries/articles/2017-01-13/13-superstitions-from-around-the-world

(N.d.-a). History.com. https://www.history.com/news/why-do-people-knock-on-wood-for-luck#:~:text=One%20common%20explanation%20traces%20the,a%20stroke%20of%20good%20luck.

(N.d.-b). Usnews.com. https://www.usnews.com/news/best-countries/articles/2017-01-13/13-superstitions-from-around-the-world

10 food superstitions. (n.d.). Walkingpalates.com. https://www.walkingpalates.com/en-UK/10-food-superstitions.php

5 superstitions about funerals and cemeteries. (n.d.). Memorial Planning. https://www.memorialplanning.com/blog/5-superstitions-about-funerals-and-cemeteries

7 crazy food superstitions to digest. (2015, February 5). Farmers' Almanac - Plan Your Day. Grow Your Life; Farmers' Almanac. https://www.farmersalmanac.com/food-superstitions-20419

7 food superstitions you must remember. (n.d.). Christopher-torrevieja.com. https://www.christopher-torrevieja.com/7-food-superstitions-you-must-remember/

8 bizarre food superstitions. (2015, November 14). Tastemade. https://www.tastemade.com/articles/8-bizarre-food-superstitions/

Ablan, D. (2014, April 16). Asbury Park Press. Asbury Park Press. https://www.app.com/story/life/food/2014/04/16/hot-cross-buns-ward-off-evil-spirits/7734891/

ArtDependence. (n.d.). ArtDependence. ArtDependence. https://www.artdependence.com/articles/symbolism-in-art-the-egg/

Arts, G. (n.d.). 18 superstitions from around the world. Google Arts & Culture. https://artsandculture.google.com/story/18-superstitions-from-around-the-world/QQIyTWmzJ9QvLg

Arts, G. (n.d.). Umbrella or parasol? Google Arts & Culture. https://artsandculture.google.com/usergallery/YAISMX_YucmALg

Athira. (2022, September 12). Walking under ladders – meaning of the superstition. Symbol Sage. https://symbolsage.com/walking-under-ladders/

benadmin, & Heath, F. (2017, April 2). Why you MUST wish on a fallen eyelash. Benito. https://benitobrowbar.com/2017/04/03/why-you-must-wish-on-a-fallen-eyelash/

Bhattacharjee, S. (2021, August 26). 7 most common superstitions of seafarers. Marine Insight. https://www.marineinsight.com/life-at-sea/7-most-common-superstitions-of-seafarers/

Brodsky, S., & Schubak, A. (2017, October 11). 55 of the strangest superstitions from around the world. Good Housekeeping. https://www.goodhousekeeping.com/life/g4489/strangest-superstitions/

Celestial Omens. (n.d.). Arizona.edu. http://ircamera.as.arizona.edu/NatSci102/NatSci/images/extomens.htm

Celestial omens. (n.d.). Imss.Fi.It. https://brunelleschi.imss.fi.it/galileopalazzostrozzi/object/CelestialOmens.html

Charbonneau, J. (2022, April 19). Garden folklore: 10 superstitions and traditions. Southern Exposure Seed Exchange | Saving the Past for the Future; Southern Exposure Seed Exchange. https://blog.southernexposure.com/2022/04/garden-folklore-10-superstitions-and-traditions/

Chinese superstitions on colors, numbers, and flowers. (2021, July 19). Han Hai Language Studio. https://www.hanhai-language.com.sg/blog/2021/7/19/chinese-superstitions-on-colours-numbers-and-flowers

Coldiron, R. (2020, September 11). Food superstitions from around the world to add to your Halloween menu. Martha Stewart. https://www.marthastewart.com/7983443/food-superstitions-from-around-world

Cookist. (2020, April 7). Bread turned upside down on the table. Do you know why tradition forbids it? Cookist. https://www.cookist.com/bread-turned-upside-down-on-the-table-do-you-know-why-tradition-forbids-it/

Cowan, D. (2021, August 11). Bad luck for wildlife: 7 Animal Superstitions - Point Defiance Zoo & Aquarium. Point Defiance Zoo & Aquarium. https://www.pdza.org/bad-luck-for-wildlife/

Difference between myth and superstition. (2015, March 28). Compare the Difference Between Similar Terms. https://www.differencebetween.com/difference-between-myth-and-vs-superstition/

Dimitar, D. (2021a, May 25). 10 strange superstitions about babies and parenting around the world (part 1). Babyology-care.com. https://babyology-care.com/blog/post/10-strange-superstitions-about-babies-and-parenting-around-the-world-part-1

Dimitar, D. (2021b, June 1). 10 strange superstitions about babies and parenting around the world (part 2). Babyology-care.com. https://babyology-care.com/blog/post/10-strange-superstitions-about-babies-and-parenting-around-the-world-part-2

Drinkwater, K., & Dagnall, N. (2018, July 2). The science of superstition – and why people believe in the unbelievable. The Conversation. http://theconversation.com/the-science-of-superstition-and-why-people-believe-in-the-unbelievable-97043

Fortune Telling History & Facts. (n.d.). Study.Com. https://study.com/academy/lesson/fortune-telling-history-facts.html

Fuller, M. (2016, August 25). The weirdest superstitions from around the world. AFAR Media. https://www.afar.com/magazine/the-weirdest-superstitions-from-around-the-world

Gallary, C. (2014, November 20). What's a Wishbone, and Why Do We Crack It? Kitchn; Apartment Therapy, LLC. https://www.thekitchn.com/what-is-a-wishbone-and-why-do-we-crack-it-ingredient-intelligence-21302

Google Arts & Culture. (n.d.). 18 Superstitions from Around the World. Google Arts & Culture. https://artsandculture.google.com/story/18-superstitions-from-around-the-world/QQIyTWmzJ9QvLg

Google Arts & Culture. (n.d.). Fortune-telling and superstition. Google Arts & Culture. https://artsandculture.google.com/story/fortune-telling-and-superstition/EgVxiGLYKrypLg

Guide, I. (2018, April 12). Superstitions about travel and good luck. Inspiration Guide; Iberostar. https://www.iberostar.com/en/inspiration-guide/lifestyle/superstitions-how-ensure-good-fortune-travels/

Hale, R. (1518014788000). What's Your Lucky (or not-so-lucky) Number? Linkedin.com. https://www.linkedin.com/pulse/whats-your-lucky-so-number-richard-hale

Harte, J. (2018). Superstitious observations: fortune-telling in English folk culture. Time and Mind, 11(1), 67–88. https://doi.org/10.1080/1751696x.2018.1433357

In honor of Friday the 13th, here are 13 bird superstitions. Have you. (2015, July 9). Audubon California. https://ca.audubon.org/news/13-bird-superstitions

Is it bad luck to open an umbrella indoors? (n.d.). Wonderopolis.org. https://wonderopolis.org/wonder/Is-It-Bad-Luck-to-Open-an-Umbrella-Indoors

Johanne. (2016, June 5). Rice. Good Luck, Symbols. https://goodlucksymbols.com/rice/

Johanne. (2021, August 31). Bread superstitions. Good Luck, Symbols. https://goodlucksymbols.com/bread-superstitions/

Johnson, S., & BA. (2021, March 11). 16 funeral superstitions from all over the world. Joincake.com. https://www.joincake.com/blog/funeral-superstitions/

KADALYS. (n.d.). Wonderful banana tree. KADALYS. https://kadalys.com/en/pages/bananier

Kelly, N. (2013, July 30). Bad-Luck Numbers that Scare Off Customers. Harvard Business Review. https://hbr.org/2013/07/the-bad-luck-numbers-that-scar

Lestz, M. (2017, January 12). Bread and bad luck: A french superstition. Margo Lestz - The Curious Rambler; Margo Lestz. https://curiousrambler.com/bread-and-bad-luck/

Lombardi, E. (2003, August 25). What's the difference between myth, folklore, and legend? ThoughtCo. https://www.thoughtco.com/defining-terms-myth-folklore-legend-735039

Lucky and unlucky numbers around the world. (n.d.). Mama Lisa's World of Children and International Culture. https://www.mamalisa.com/blog/lucky-and-unlucky-numbers/

Mandov, G. (2015, July 1). How to read signs and omens. Inner Outer Peace. https://innerouterpeace.com/how-to-read-signs-and-omens-in-everyday-life/

Martin, G. (n.d.). "Why does bread always fall buttered side down?" - the meaning and origin of this phrase. Phrasefinder. https://www.phrases.org.uk/meanings/butter-side-down.html

Meno, A. (2023, January 26). 15 mystifying superstitions about babies and pregnancy from around the world. Cracked.com. https://www.cracked.com/image-pictofact-9666-15-mystifying-superstitions-about-babies-and-pregnancy-from-around-the-world

MIniac, M. (2015, January 3). Lucky and unlucky numbers from around the world. Sottypong-Review's Site. https://sottyreview.wordpress.com/2015/01/04/lucky-and-unlucky-numbers-from-around-the-world/

Mirror myths & superstitions. (2020, February 5). Two-Way Mirrors. https://www.twowaymirrors.com/mirror-superstitions/

Mulu, R. (2021, June 21). Symbolism and meaning of salt. Symbol Sage. https://symbolsage.com/salt-symbolism-and-meaning/

Numerology: Lucky & unlucky numbers. (2013, March 3). SchoolWorkHelper. https://schoolworkhelper.net/numerology-lucky-unlucky-numbers/

Ottermann, B. (2011, May 22). 13 food superstitions. Health24. https://www.news24.com/health24/diet-and-nutrition/healthy-foods/13-food-superstitions-20120721

Patch, F. (2019, February 19). 40 Filipino Superstitions that You Need to Know during Funerals and Wakes. Flower Patch - Online Flower Delivery Phillippines |; Flower Patch - Online Flower Delivery Phillippines. https://flowerpatchdelivery.com/blog/40-filipino-superstitions-funerals-and-wakes/

Petrova, E. (2020, February 16). 5 curious bread superstitions you wouldn't expect. Hellenic Grocery. https://hellenicgrocery.co.uk/blogs/blog/5-curious-bread-superstitions-wouldnt-expect

Queaño, P. (2016, April 29). 10 food superstitions in 10 countries. Opodo Travel Blog; Opodo. https://www.opodo.co.uk/blog/food-superstitions/

Raga, S. (2016, May 9). 14 Good Luck Superstitions from Around the World. Mental Floss. https://www.mentalfloss.com/article/79409/14-good-luck-superstitions-around-world

Raymond, C. (n.d.). 13 death and dying superstitions. Funeralhelpcenter.com. https://www.funeralhelpcenter.com/13-death-dying-superstitions/

Reum, Y. (n.d.). Symbolism of mirrors as the first step of individuation and self-awareness. E-jsst.org. https://www.e-jsst.org/upload/jsst-9-1-45.pdf

Rhys, D. (2022a, August 2). 10 superstitions about mirrors. Symbol Sage. https://symbolsage.com/superstitions-about-mirrors/

Rhys, D. (2022b, September 29). Opening an umbrella indoors – how do you reverse its effects? Symbol Sage. https://symbolsage.com/opening-umbrella-indoors-bad-luck/

Saladino, E. (2018, March 6). Why you should never toast with water in your glass. VinePair. https://vinepair.com/articles/bad-luck-toast-water-navy/

Sprankles, J. (2018, June 25). 10 times the celebrity death rule of threes actually happened. SheKnows. https://www.sheknows.com/entertainment/slideshow/9629/celebrity-death-rule-of-threes/9/

Stanek, A. (2022, March 21). 7 horseshoe superstitions still practiced today. Horsey Hooves. https://horseyhooves.com/horseshoe-superstitions/

Symbols, colors, numbers, superstitions, and food. (2019, May 6). Germany Culture Analysis. https://germany789125405.wordpress.com/symbols-colors-numbers-superstitions-and-food/

Tempera, J. (2022, September 14). How to find your lucky numbers in numerology and what each one means, according to experts. Women's Health. https://www.womenshealthmag.com/life/a41124320/lucky-numbers/

Tetrault, S., & BA. (2020, June 5). 17 death superstitions from around the world. Joincake.com. https://www.joincake.com/blog/death-superstitions/

The College of Psychic Studies : Enlighten : Guide to scrying. (n.d.). The College of Psychic Studies. https://www.collegeofpsychicstudies.co.uk/enlighten/guide-to-scrying/

The meaning and symbol of Yogurt in dream. (n.d.). Onlinedreamdictionary.com. https://www.onlinedreamdictionary.com/4389-the-meaning-and-symbol-of-yogurt-in-dream/

Thirteen Animal Superstitions. (n.d.). Advanced Integrated Pest Management. https://www.advancedipm.com/blog/2015/february/thirteen-animal-superstitions/

Timmons, J. (2023, January 5). How To Do A Basic Tarot Reading For Yourself Or A Friend. Mindbodygreen. https://www.mindbodygreen.com/articles/how-to-do-a-basic-tarot-reading

Trujillo, N. (2015, March 19). 9 unbelievable pregnancy superstitions from around the world. Woman's Day. https://www.womansday.com/relationships/family-friends/g1783/pregnancy-superstitions/?slide=1

Turner, B. (2015, July 17). 13 superstitions about numbers. HowStuffWorks. https://people.howstuffworks.com/13-superstitions-about-numbers.htm

Tuttle, R. (2013, February 7). Symbolism of colors and their superstitions. Odd Random Thoughts. https://oddrandomthoughts.com/symbolism-of-colors-and-their-superstitions/

Tuttle, R. (2013, May 19). Superstitions about bread and the baker's dozen. Odd Random Thoughts. https://oddrandomthoughts.com/bread-in-bakery-myths-and-superstitions-about-bread/

Vergara, V. (2021, May 20). 9 superstitions associated with plants and gardens. https://the-line-up.com/; Open Road Media. https://the-line-up.com/plant-and-garden-superstitions

Verma, V. (2020, October 28). 6 popular garden superstitions that you should be aware of. Winni - Celebrate Relations. https://www.winni.in/celebrate-relations/6-popular-garden-superstitions-that-you-should-be-aware-of/

Wagner, S. (n.d.). Try Automatic Writing and Get Messages From Beyond. LiveAbout. https://www.liveabout.com/how-to-practice-automatic-writing-2593046

Webeck, D. (2017, January 18). 13 pregnancy superstitions from across the globe. Stuff. https://www.stuff.co.nz/life-style/parenting/pregnancy/88535413/13-pregnancy-superstitions-from-across-the-globe

Why onion? (n.d.). Onion-Collective. https://www.onioncollective.co.uk/why-onion

Why should you eat garlic empty stomach? (2015, April 18). The Times of India; Times Of India. https://timesofindia.indiatimes.com/life-style/health-fitness/home-remedies/why-you-should-eat-garlic-empty-stomach/articleshow/46957694.cms

Wigington, P. (n.d.). Methods of Divination. Learn Religions. https://www.learnreligions.com/methods-of-divination-2561764

wikiHow. (2011, November 10). How to Get Rid of Bad Luck. WikiHow. https://www.wikihow.com/Get-Rid-of-Bad-Luck

Wolchover, N., & Dutfield, S. (2022, January 28). The meaning of colors: How 8 colors became symbolic. Livescience.com; Live Science. https://www.livescience.com/33523-color-symbolism-meanings.html A folklore survey of county Clare: Animal and plant superstitions. (n.d.). Clarelibrary.Ie. https://www.clarelibrary.ie/eolas/coclare/folklore/folklore_survey/chapter17.htm

Wolfe, S. E. (2021, April 6). Divination Methods for Beginners. Green Witch Living. A beginner's guide to reading tea leaves. Hello Lunch Lady. https://hellolunchlady.com.au/blogs/blog/beginners-guide-reading-tea-leaves

Xing, J. (2022, August 11). 60 common superstitions that people around the world believe. YourTango. https://www.yourtango.com/self/common-superstitions-from-around-world-people-believe

Xing, J. (2022, January 24). Fish symbolism & spiritual meanings of seeing fish. YourTango. https://www.yourtango.com/2020335336/what-spiritual-meaning-fish

(N.d.). Poddtoppen.Se. https://poddtoppen.se/podcast/1481017209/keeping-her-keys/how-to-create-an-altar-of-hekate

(N.d.-a). Pdfgoes.com. https://pdfgoes.com/download/4015389-Hekate%20Liminal%20Rites%20A%20Study%20Of%20The%20Rituals%20Magic%20And%20Symbols%20Of%20The%20Torch%20Bearing%20Triple%20Goddess%20Of%20The%20Crossroads.pdf

(N.d.-b). Pdfgoes.com. https://pdfgoes.com/download/3533918-The%20Temple%20Of%20Hekate%20Exploring%20The%20Goddess%20Hekate%20Through%20Ritual%20Meditation%20And%20Divination.pdf

"HECATE (Hekate) - Greek Goddess of Witchcraft, Magic & Ghosts." n.d. Theoi.com. https://www.theoi.com/Khthonios/Hekate.html.

"Hekate's Deipnon." n.d. Hellenion.org. https://www.hellenion.org/festivals/hekates-deipnon/.

"Honor the Queen of the Night, Hecate on Her Day." n.d. Campaign-archive.com. https://us20.campaign-archive.com/?u=08b2468195beb1c529a55ee1f&id=ad908f9c6a.

"Noumenia." n.d. Hellenion.org. https://www.hellenion.org/festivals/noumenia/.

ASTERIA. (n.d.). Theoi.com. https://www.theoi.com/Titan/TitanisAsteria.html

Bel, Bekah Evie. 2016. "Observing Hekates Deipnon." Hearth Witch Down Under. June 13, 2016. https://www.patheos.com/blogs/hearthwitchdownunder/2016/06/observing-hekates-deipnon.html.

Brannen, Cyndi. 2020. "Leaning into Hekate's Crossroads during Difficult Times." Keeping Her Keys. May 20, 2020. https://www.patheos.com/blogs/keepingherkeys/2020/05/hekates-crossroads/.

BUST Magazine. (2020, August 26). Let the ancient spirit of Hekate awaken your inner dark goddess. Bust.com. https://bust.com/living/197579-hekate-dark-goddess-spirit-witch-empower.html

Cartwright, M. (2017). Hecate. World History Encyclopedia. http://worldhistory.org/Hecate/

Cartwright, M. (2017). Hecate. World History Encyclopedia. https://www.worldhistory.org/Hecate/

Cosette. 2021. "Observing the Deipnon and Noumenia, Hecate's Monthly Rituals." Divine Hours Priestess | Tarot Reader (blog). Cosette. October 21, 2021. https://cosettepaneque.com/observing-the-deipnon-and-noumenia-hecates-monthly-rituals/.

Creating an altar – the covenant of hekate (CoH). (n.d.). Hekatecovenant.com. http://hekatecovenant.com/rite-of-her-sacred-fires/useful-info/creating-an-altar/

d'Este, S. (2020, August 24). Hekate's wheel & the iynx wheel. Adamantine Muse. https://www.patheos.com/blogs/adamantinemuse/2020/08/hekates-wheel-the-iynx-wheel/

Dharni, A. (2020, August 12). Queen Of The Night flowers blooming in A time-lapse video is nature at its best. India Times. https://www.indiatimes.com/trending/environment/queen-of-the-night-flowers-blooming-time-lapse-video-520110.html

Erickson, J. (2019, June 6). Herbs of Hecate. Medium. https://janerickson.medium.com/herbs-of-hecate-8399d08ca8c6

Fields, K. (2020, January 21). Hecate: 15 ways to work with the goddess of witchcraft. Otherworldly Oracle; FIELDS CREATIVE CONSULTING. https://otherworldlyoracle.com/hecate-goddess/

Fields, K. (2020, January 5). Key Magic, Myth, and a Lock & Key Spell for Protection. Otherworldly Oracle. https://otherworldlyoracle.com/key-magic/

Greek Olympians. (n.d.). Mythopedia. https://mythopedia.com/topics/greek-olympians

Greenberg, M. (2021, March 22). Hecate Greek goddess of witchcraft: A complete guide (2022). MythologySource; Mike Greenberg, PhD. https://mythologysource.com/hecate-greek-goddess/

HECATE (hekate) - Greek goddess of witchcraft, magic & ghosts. (n.d.). Theoi.com. https://www.theoi.com/Khthonios/Hekate.html

Hecate. (n.d.). Hellenicaworld.com. https://www.hellenicaworld.com/Greece/Mythology/en/Hecate.html

Hecate. (n.d.). Mythopedia. https://mythopedia.com/topics/hecate

Hecate: Triple-bodied Greek goddess of witchcraft and keeper of keys. (2022, October 6). Ancient Origins. https://www.ancient-origins.net/myths-legends-europe/hecate-0010707

Hecate's wheel, strophalos meaning, symbolism, origin and uses. (2021, September 29). Symbols and Meanings - Your Ultimate Guide for Symbolism. https://symbolsandmeanings.net/hecates-wheel-strophalos-meaning-symbolism-origin-uses/

Hekate's Open Pathway Spell. (n.d.). Tumblr. https://hekateanwitchcraft.tumblr.com/post/625740934293913600/this-spell-is-similar-to-a-road-opening-spell-but

Hekatean Home Protection. (n.d.). Tumblr. https://hekateanwitchcraft.tumblr.com/post/631719732022771712/hekatean-home-protection

hekateanwitchcraft. (n.d.). Tumblr. https://hekateanwitchcraft.tumblr.com/post/139478162262/hi-i-thought-your-posts-about-your-epithet-for

Huanaco, F. (2021, June 8). Hecate: Goddess symbols, correspondences, myth & offerings. Spells8. https://spells8.com/lessons/hecate-goddess-symbols/

Jason. (n.d.). Mythopedia. https://mythopedia.com/topics/jason

Kabir, S. R. (2022, September 27). Hecate: The goddess of witchcraft in Greek mythology. History Cooperative; The History Cooperative. https://historycooperative.org/hecate-goddess-of-witchcraft/

Keys, K. H. (n.d.). Hekate: Altars and offerings. Keeping Her Keys. https://keepingherkeys.com/blog/f/creating-altars-and-shrines

Keys, K. H. (n.d.). Hekate: The Keeper of keys. Keeping Her Keys. https://keepingherkeys.com/blog/f/hekate-the-keeper-of-keys

Kyteler, E. (n.d.). Herbal offerings for Hecate. Eclecticwitchcraft.com. https://eclecticwitchcraft.com/hecate-herbal-offerings/

Mackay, D. (2021, June 27). Everything you need to know about Hecate (maiden, mother, crone). TheCollector. https://www.thecollector.com/hecate-goddess-magic-witchcraft/

Meeting Hekate at Her Crossroads - Guided Meditation. (n.d.). SoundCloud. https://soundcloud.com/thewitchespath/meeting-hekate-at-her-crossroads-guided-meditation

My Hekate Oil Recipe. (n.d.). Tumblr. https://hekateanwitchcraft.tumblr.com/post/627289683874988032/my-hekate-oil-recipe

Nightly Prayer to Hekate. (n.d.). Tumblr. https://hekateanwitchcraft.tumblr.com/post/136232812112/nightly-prayer-to-hekate

PHOEBE (phoibe) - Greek Titan goddess of the Delphi oracle. (n.d.). Theoi.com. https://www.theoi.com/Titan/TitanisPhoibe.html

Prayer of Devotion for Hekate. (n.d.). Tumblr. https://hekateanwitchcraft.tumblr.com/post/158919116652/prayer-of-devotion-for-hekate

Rhys, D. (2020a, August 20). Hecate's Wheel symbol – origins and meaning. Symbol Sage. https://symbolsage.com/hecate-wheel-symbolism-and-meaning/

Rhys, D. (2020b, September 9). Hecate – Greek goddess of magic and spells. Symbol Sage. https://symbolsage.com/greek-goddess-of-magic/

Signs from Hekate. (n.d.). Tumblr. https://hekateanwitchcraft.tumblr.com/post/629191173466112000/signs-from-hekate

Small Ways to Incorporate Hekate Worship/Devotion into Your Everyday Life. (n.d.). Tumblr. https://hekateanwitchcraft.tumblr.com/post/630069116650356736/small-ways-to-incorporate-hekate-worshipdevotion

Starting with Hekate. (n.d.). Tumblr. https://hekateanwitchcraft.tumblr.com/post/141027130657/starting-with-hekate

Tarotpugs, /. (2017, October 28). Hekate tarot spread. TarotPugs. https://tarotpugs.com/2017/10/28/hekate-tarot-spread/

The Editors of Encyclopedia Britannica. (2023). Hecate. In Encyclopedia Britannica.

The Eldrum Tree. (2016, January 20). Hecate's herbs – part one. Eldrum.co.uk. https://eldrum.co.uk/2016/01/20/hecates-herbs-part-one/

The orphic hymn to Hecate Ækáti. (n.d.). HellenicGods.org. https://www.hellenicgods.org/the-orphic-hymn-to-hecate-aekati---hekate

Thompson, E. (2019, April 30). How to Make a Crystal Grid, a Step-by-Step Guide. Almanac Supply Co. https://almanacsupplyco.com/blogs/articles/how-to-make-a-crystal-grid

Turnbull, L. (2022, October 27). Hecate: Greek goddess of The Crossroads. Goddess Gift; The Goddess Path. https://goddessgift.com/goddesses/hecate/

Uk, C. L. [@charmedlifeuk3341]. (2021, February 6). Hecate meditation- guided journey to goddess Hecate's cave to receive her guidance.

Caro, T. (2021, July 31). Creating a powerful Altar for Hecate (a quick DIY guide). Magickal Spot. https://magickalspot.com/altar-for-hecate/

Welch, M. (2021, August 29). Kidnapped! The shocking story of Persephone and Hades. Definitelygreece.Gr; Rania Kalogirou. https://www.definitelygreece.com/the-story-of-persephone-and-hades/

What is Hekatean Witchcraft? (n.d.). Tumblr. https://hekateanwitchcraft.tumblr.com/post/631201126976471040/what-is-hekatean-witchcraft

Willett, J., & Tucson, T. I. (2019, June 22). 5 things to know about the mysterious queen of cacti, the night-blooming cereus. This Is Tucson